Growth-Oriented Entrepreneurship

Growth-Oriented Entrepreneurship

Alan S. Gutterman

BEP BUSINESS EXPERT PRESS

Growth-Oriented Entrepreneurship

First published in 2018 by
Business Expert Press, LLC
222 East 46th Street, New York, NY 10017
www.businessexpertpress.com

ISBN-13: 978-1-94897-659-6 (paperback)
ISBN-13: 978-1-94897-660-2 (e-book)

Business Expert Press Entrepreneurship and Small Business Management Collection

Collection ISSN: 1946-5653 (print)
Collection ISSN: 1946-5661 (electronic)

Cover and interior design by Exeter Premedia Services Private Ltd., Chennai, India

First edition: 2018

10 9 8 7 6 5 4 3 2 1

Printed in the United States of America.

Abstract

A number of different methods have been used to describe "growth-oriented entrepreneurship"; however, there is a consensus that there is a particularly desirable form of entrepreneurship that seeks to create and scale up businesses that will drive productivity growth, create new employment, increase innovation, promote business internationalization, and achieve sustainable economic growth. "Innovation" is a condition of growth-oriented entrepreneurship that includes both the development and commercialization of new products and services and the development and implementation of new or improved processes that enhance productivity or reduce costs associated with manufacturing or distributing existing products. Innovation involves firms pursuing distinctive business strategies and doing new things in new ways to increase productivity, product development, sales and profitability, including finding and developing new ways of identifying the needs of new and existing customers and making and marketing products that satisfy those needs. The goal of the launch phase for growth-oriented entrepreneurial ventures is to reach the point of "scale up" and common goals and activities associated with the launch phase include market disruption and penetration; gaining access to capital and markets and mentorship opportunities; organizational growth through management capacity, systems, resources (i.e., people, product, and assets) management; embedding organizational culture; development of stakeholder relationships; monitoring and evaluation; and governance and reporting. This book provides an extensive introduction to research on growth-oriented entrepreneurship and continues with an assessment of attempts to create the appropriate framework conditions for growth-oriented entrepreneurship to flourish and sustain including financial support; government policies; government programs; education and training; research and development transfer; commercial and professional infrastructure; internal market openness; access to physical infrastructure; cultural and social norms; and protection of intellectual property rights. The final chapter looks at growth-oriented entrepreneurs in practice as they work to launch and growth emerging companies. This book is a unique compendium of research and analysis on a dynamic and important segment of entrepreneurship and will be useful to entrepreneurs, academics, and policymakers.

Keywords

emerging companies, entrepreneurship, high-impact entrepreneurship, innovation clusters, knowledge-based entrepreneurship, opportunity-based entrepreneurship

Contents

CHAPTER 1

Growth-Oriented Entrepreneurship

Introduction

Entrepreneurship is a popular topic for researchers and policymakers around the world and much of the work in the area does not distinguish new businesses by size or strategy. However, it is now widely acknowledged that a sub-class of entrepreneurs, often referred to as "growth-oriented entrepreneurs" or "high-growth entrepreneurs," can be identified and distinguished by their aspirations relating to job creation, innovation, and internationalization, all of which have been positively related to the economic development that is important to so many governments.[1] Acs and Szerb, the creators of the Global Entrepreneurship and Development Index (GEDI), argued that international rankings of entrepreneurial activities in various countries should place more weight and importance on the amount of entrepreneurial activity directed toward innovation, high-impact entrepreneurship and globalization focused their research on international entrepreneurship and "the efforts of the early-stage entrepreneur to introduce new products and services, develop new production processes, penetrate foreign markets, substantially increase the number of firm employees, and finance the business with either formal or informal venture capital, or both."[2]

---

[1] Amoros, J., and N. Bosma. 2014. *Global Entrepreneurship Monitor 2013 Global Report: Fifteen Years of Assessing Entrepreneurship Across the Globe*, 37–41.

[2] Acs, Z., and L. Szerb. June 2010. "The Global Entrepreneurship and Development Index (GEDI)." Paper Presented at Summer Conference 2010 on "Opening Up Innovation: Strategy, Organization and Technology." Imperial College London Business School.

As to what constitutes a "high-growth firm," Audretsch offered several definitions.[3] For example, the 2007 OECD-Eurostat Manual on Business Demography Statistics defined the term to include:

All enterprises with average annualized growth greater than 20 percent per annum, over a three-year period, and with 10 or more employees at the beginning of the observation period. Growth is thus measured by the number of employees and by turnover.

The same source explained "gazelle firms" to be "[a]ll enterprises up to five years old with average annualized growth greater than 20 percent per annum over a three-year period, and with 10 or more employees at the beginning of the observation period." When Delta Economics surveyed "growth oriented" entrepreneurs in BRICSA countries, the US and Europe, it limited its survey to entrepreneurs running relatively young businesses (between 2 and 10 years old) that had turned over a minimum of $300,000 after the second year of trading and found that "growth oriented" businesses shared several common features: high growth rate in turnover; average employment of around 25 people and expectations of doubling the size of the workforce within three years; high likelihood that initial financing came from self-investment, usually from savings; some level of innovation in the way in which they approached their markets, product differentiation, or research and development; and international orientation.[4] For Llisterri and Garcia-Alba, "new, dynamic ventures" in Latin America, Asia, and Europe were "firms between three and 10 years old that had grown to employ at least 15 workers, and no more than 100, during the study" and which were likely to engage in export activities and

---

[3] Audretsch. D. March 28, 2012. *Determinants of High-Growth Entrepreneurship Report Prepared for the OECD/DBA International Workshop on High-Growth Firms: Local Policies and Local Determinants*. Copenhagen.

[4] The Association of Chartered Certified Accountants July, High-growth SMEs: understanding the leaders of the recovery (July 2012) (based on data and analysis provided by Delta Economics in "Challenges and Opportunities for Growth and Sustainability").

compete on innovation (i.e., offering differentiated products or services) rather than price.[5]

As for characteristics of growth-oriented entrepreneurs, Audretsch noted that there did not appear to be significant differences in the educational background of the founders of the dynamic and less dynamic companies. In most cases, they had attained high education levels and their college degrees had provided them with important technical knowledge, especially for the dynamic entrepreneurs; however, the educational system did little to transfer other skills necessary for successful entrepreneurship. Dynamic entrepreneurs appeared to have distinctly different learning processes for entrepreneurship than their counterparts among the less dynamic companies. For example, the previous work experiences of dynamic entrepreneurs provided significant advantages in terms of gathering information on business ideas and learning the skills necessary to commercialize those ideas. In addition, dynamic entrepreneurs were better able to establish and mine networks of relationships that provided them with valuable support on such things as identifying business opportunities, accessing funds, forging relationships with executives at larger companies and obtaining access to information and non-financial resources such as raw materials or facilities. Delta found that the top four drivers in motivating growth-oriented entrepreneurs worldwide were in order: following a dream; taking advantage of a market opportunity; getting autonomy over the entrepreneur's time; and "making a lot of money."[6] While growth is an important facet of growth-oriented entrepreneurship, recognition has also been given to smaller firms that had opportunities to grow, and grow quickly, yet decided that while growth was a sign of health it was better to focus on "other, non-financial priorities as well, such as

[5] Llisterri, J., and J. Garcia-Alba. 2008. *HGSMEs in Latin American Emerging Economies.* The paper was prepared for "The OECD Kansas City Workshop," Session III. "From Invention to the Market Place: Acquiring knowledge and intellectual assets: The interaction between large firms and small business in the fast growth process."

[6] The Association of Chartered Certified Accountants, High-Growth SMEs: understanding the Leaders of the Recovery (July 2012) (based on data and analysis provided by Delta Economics in "Challenges and Opportunities for Growth and Sustainability").

being great at what they do, creating great places to work, providing great service to customers, making great contributions to their communities and finding great ways to lead lives."[7]

Growth-oriented Entrepreneurship

A number of different methods have been used to describe "growth-oriented entrepreneurship"; however, there is a consensus that there is a particularly desirable form of entrepreneurship that seeks to create and scale up businesses that will drive productivity growth, create new employment, increase innovation, promote business internationalization, and achieve sustainable economic growth.

Criterion for growth-oriented entrepreneurship can be understood from the following descriptions:

- "Knowledge-based entrepreneurship" is entrepreneurship in the context of medium and high technology industries, both in the manufacturing and service sectors as well. Distinguishing factors include the sophistication or intensity of technology involved, level of education, and product/service uniqueness.
- "Innovation" is a condition of growth-oriented entrepreneurship that includes both the development and commercialization of new products and services and the development and implementation of new or improved processes that enhance productivity or reduce costs associated with manufacturing or distributing existing products. Innovation involves firms pursuing distinctive business strategies and doing new things in new ways to increase productivity, product development, sales and profitability, including finding and developing new ways of identifying the needs of new and existing customers and making and marketing products that satisfy those needs.
- "Opportunity-based entrepreneurship" focuses on the motives of the entrepreneur and includes entrepreneurship undertaken to take advantage of a business opportunity. The key characteristic among opportunity-based entrepreneurs is their acknowledgment that they made a voluntary career choice to pursue an entrepreneurial path.
- "Genuine entrepreneurship" describes situations where individuals start businesses with the goal of generating sufficient income so that a portion of it can be reinvested in order to underwrite business growth and development.
- "High-impact entrepreneurship" combines various characteristics and goals of entrepreneurial activity including innovation (i.e., development of new technologies, products and/or services and/or development of new production processes), penetration of foreign markets and globalization of overall business activities, an objective of substantially increasing the number of firm employees, and financing the business with risk capital.

Relevant metrics for growth-oriented entrepreneurship include changes in sales, assets, employment, productivity, profits and profit margins.

The goal of the launch phase for growth-oriented entrepreneurial ventures is to reach the point of "scale up" and common goals and activities associated with the

---

[7] Burlingham, B. February 8, 2016. "Best Small Companies." *Forbes*, 86.

launch phase include market disruption and penetration; gaining access to capital and markets and mentorship opportunities; organizational growth through management capacity, systems, resources (i.e., people, product and assets) management; embedding organizational culture; development of stakeholder relationships; monitoring and evaluation; and governance and reporting.

Finally, framework conditions for growth-oriented entrepreneurship to flourish and sustain include financial support; government policies; government programs; education and training; research and development transfer; commercial and professional infrastructure; internal market openness; access to physical infrastructure; cultural and social norms; and protection of intellectual property rights.

Global Entrepreneurship Monitor

The Global Entrepreneurship Monitor (GEM) is a partnership between the London Business School and Babson College that administers a comprehensive research program to produce annual assessments of national levels of entrepreneurial activity. The project was first launched in 1999, when it covered just 10 countries, and has since grown to cover as many as 85 countries in subsequent years and is recognized as the largest ongoing study of entrepreneurial dynamics in the world. The main objectives of the GEM program are measurement of differences in the level of entrepreneurial activity between countries, uncovering the factors that lead to appropriate levels of entrepreneurship and making suggestions for policies that may lead to enhancement of national levels of entrepreneurial activity.[8]

The GEM is based on a conceptual model of the institutional environment and its effect on entrepreneurship. The model recognizes the importance of the social, cultural, and political context in which entrepreneurial activities occur and assumes that these contextual factors influence three sets of conditions: basic requirements, which include institutions, infrastructure, macroeconomic stability, health, and primary education; "efficiency enhancers," which include higher education, goods and labor

---

[8] For further discussion of the GEM, see "Research on entrepreneurship." In "Entrepreneurship: A Library of Resources for Sustainable Entrepreneurs" prepared and distributed by the Sustainable Entrepreneurship Project (www.seproject.org).

market efficiency, financial market sophistication, technological readiness, and market size; and the "entrepreneurial framework conditions" (EFCs).

Entrepreneurship itself is measured in the GEM surveys by looking at the entrepreneurship profile of prospective and actual entrepreneurs, including their attitudes, activities, and aspirations; and at the entrepreneurship process itself. Data is collected through adult population surveys in all of the countries that are used to measure individual involvement in venture creation, identify the motives of entrepreneurs, measure the aspirations of entrepreneurs with respect to pursuing high growth and/or activities in foreign markets and understand the societal climate for entrepreneurship.

GEM is concerned with all types of entrepreneurship and "potential entrepreneurs," who are described as persons who see opportunities in their areas, believe they have the abilities and resources to start businesses to pursue those opportunities and who are not deterred by fear of failure in pursuing those opportunities. Potential entrepreneurs who go on to start new businesses are referred to as "new business owners" in the GEM surveys and are tracked for up to three and one-half years after they first go into business. No size or strategy conditions are imposed on "new business owners"; however, the GEM researchers have recognized the special impact of growth-oriented entrepreneurs, who can be identified and distinguished by their aspirations relating to job creation, innovation, and internationalization, all of which are measured and compared within the survey methodology used by GEM.[9]

---

[9] The discussion in this section is adapted from Amoros, J., and N. Bosma. 2014. *Global Entrepreneurship Monitor 2013 Global Report: Fifteen Years of Assessing Entrepreneurship Across the Globe*, 37–41. Job creation, innovation, and internationalization have been positively associated with economic development (see e.g., Wong, P., Y. Ho, and E. Autio. 2005. "Entrepreneurship, Innovation and Economic Growth: Evidence from GEM Data." *Small Business Economics* 24, no. 3, p. 335; Bosma, N. 2011. "Entrepreneurship, Urbanization Economies and Productivity of European Regions." In *Handbook of Research on Entrepreneurship and Regional Development*, ed. M.F. Fritsch, 107. Cheltenham, UK; Northampton, MA, USA: Edward Elgar; and Wennekers, S., A. Van Stel, M. Carree, and A. Thurik. 2010. "The Relationship Between Entrepreneurship and Economic Development: Is It U-shaped?" *Foundations and Trends in Entrepreneurship* 6, no. 3, p. 167).

Job Creation

GEM measures growth orientation by focusing on plans and expectations of the entrepreneur with respect to creation of new jobs. GEM surveys early-stage entrepreneurs to learn how many employees (other than the owners) they currently have and expect to have in the next five years. Amoros and Bosma explained that "this measure relates to the entrepreneur's expectations about the potential for their businesses, but in most cases this is also reflecting their ambitions to grow their ventures," which is important because research has shown that while the goals for job creation may not be realized success is achieved without having expectations or ambitions for growth.[10]

The results of GEM surveys are presented with three levels of projected growth for new businesses: low (0–5 new employees in five years); medium (6–19 new employees), or high (20+ new employees). Amoros and Bosma noted that while the percentage of adult persons in Sub-Saharan Africa engaged in some way in launching a new business was higher than anywhere else in the world, growth aspirations among early-stage entrepreneurs in Sub-Saharan Africa were quite limited: more than 80 percent of the entrepreneurs indicating they expect to add less than five employees within the next five years and only 4 percent projecting 20 or more new jobs. On the other hand, while percentage of adult persons engaged in entrepreneurship in North America and Europe was much lower than in Sub-Saharan Africa, more than 10 percent of the early-stage entrepreneurs in those regions had high growth expectations (i.e., 20+ new employees in five years).

Innovation

Innovation orientation is measured and valued by GEM because it is perceived as being the foundation of structural renewal over the long term. Amoros and Bosma explained that innovation represented "the

---

[10] Stam, E., N. Bosma, A. Van Witteloostuijn, J. De Jong, S. Bogaert, N. Edwards, and F. Jaspers. 2012. *Ambitious Entrepreneurship. A Review of the Academic Literature and New Directions for Public Policy, (AWT Report 41)*. The Hague: AWT.

perceived extent to which an entrepreneur's product or service is new to some or all customers and where few or no other businesses offer the same product." GEM surveys focused on two separate, albeit closely related, measures of innovation: the percentage of adult persons engaged in entrepreneurial activity that declare they have a product or service that is a novelty (new) for all or some or their consumers; and the percentage of such persons that declare they are new in the market with few or no other businesses that offer the same product or service. Not surprisingly, the average level of innovation in a geographic region increases along the overall level of economic development in that region. Amoros and Bosma reported that North America and the European Union had the largest proportions on both measures and that high proportions of innovative products were also seen in Asian countries such as Japan, Korea, and China. Among the emerging markets, high rates of both new products and new markets were found in Columbia, Chile, South Africa, and Taiwan.

Internationalization

Finally, the interest of GEM in international orientation reflects the reality of an increasingly global economy and the ability of even the smallest firms to leverage technological tools to broaden the scope of their businesses beyond their domestic market, a path that is particularly important for firms in economies with smaller internal markets. GEM recognizes for categories of early-stage entrepreneurs relating to their degree of internationalization: from 0 percent of their customers living outside the origin country, to high degrees of internationalization with 75 percent or more of their customers living outside the country. Amoros and Bosma reported that countries in the European Union had a high proportion of entrepreneurs with at least 25 percent of their customers living outside their countries, a result they attributed in part to the tradition of international commerce among those countries and their geographic proximity. On the other hand, much lower proportions of international-oriented entrepreneurs were found among the countries in the Latin American and Sub-Saharan economies. Amoros and Bosma emphasized three key observations regarding trends seen in the internationalization data[11]:

- China, India, Indonesia, Thailand, Brazil, Mexico, and Russia, all economies with large populations and large land mass, have very low rates of internationalization among their early-stage entrepreneurs.
- Early-stage entrepreneurs in the US, the largest market in the world, exhibited medium internationalization rates, a reflection of the fact that while such entrepreneurs were attracted to foreign markets they also did not want to neglect their own large and diverse domestic market with customers that have relatively high disposable incomes. In addition, competitive intensity is high in the US and demands significant attention and resources from early-stage entrepreneurs attempting to gain a foothold in their internal market.
- Several countries with relatively small local markets had high levels of internationalization among their early-stage entrepreneurs. For example, entrepreneurs in countries such as Israel, Luxemburg, and Singapore expanded aggressively into foreign markets with their highly innovation orientation in services and technology-based products. Smaller countries in the European Union had high levels of international orientation due to their traditional emphasis on trade and their need and ability to participate in their regional trading arrangement.

Global Entrepreneurship and Development Index

Acs and Szerb, the creators of the GEDI believed that the GEM project and its focus on the business formation process in a large number of countries, while impressive and valuable, fell short due to its failure to incorporate

---

[11] See also Kelley, D., S. Singer, and M. Herrington. 2012. *Global Entrepreneurship Monitor: 2011 Global Report*. Babson Park, MA: Global Entrepreneurship Research Association.

the different impacts of new businesses and its ranking of countries based primarily on the number of new businesses without regard to their success from a financial perspective or in terms of job creation, improving the local knowledge base and increasing the level of development and innovation.[12] The GEDI captures the contextual features of entrepreneurship by focusing on three broad areas: entrepreneurial attitudes (i.e., a society's basic attitudes toward entrepreneurship through education and social stability); entrepreneurial activity (i.e., what individuals are actually doing to improve the quality of human resources and technological efficiency); and entrepreneurial aspirations (i.e., the amount of entrepreneurial activity directed toward innovation, high-impact entrepreneurship, and globalization).[13] The third area, "entrepreneurial aspirations," focuses specifically on qualitative elements of entrepreneurial activity (e.g., skills, innovation, and high growth) and places greater weight and importance on "the efforts of the early-stage entrepreneur to introduce new products and services, develop new production processes, penetrate foreign markets, substantially increase the number of firm employees, and finance the business with either formal or informal venture capital, or both."[14]

---

[12] Acs, Z., and L. Szerb. 2010. "The Global Entrepreneurship and Development Index (GEDI)." Paper Presented at Summer Conference 2010 on "Opening Up Innovation: Strategy, Organization and Technology," Imperial College London Business School. For further discussion of the GEDI, see "Research on Entrepreneurship" in "Entrepreneurship: A Library of Resources for Sustainable Entrepreneurs" prepared and distributed by the Sustainable Entrepreneurship Project (www.seproject.org).

[13] Acs, Z., and L. Szerb. 2010. *Global Entrepreneurship and the United States.* Washington, DC: US Small Business Administration Office of Advocacy. http://sba.gov/content/global-entrepreneurship-and-united-states (accessed April 30, 2011).

[14] Acs, Z., and E. Autio. 2010. "The Global Entrepreneurship and Development Index: A Brief Explanation." www.imperial.ac.uk/business-school (accessed April 30, 2011). One of the institutional variables used by Acs and Szerb was "business strategy" and referred to "the ability of companies to pursue distinctive strategies, which involves differentiated positioning and innovative means of production and service delivery." See Acs, Z., and L. Szerb. 2010. "The Global Entrepreneurship and Development Index (GEDI)." Paper Presented at Summer Conference

Acs and Szerb believed that "entrepreneurship" should be seen as a dynamic interaction of the three areas mentioned above—attitudes, activity, and aspirations—and should be clearly distinguished from small businesses, self-employment, craftsmanship, and "usual businesses."[15] They felt that it was essential to acknowledge that certain new businesses were more impactful than others with respect to key metrics for economic development such as job creation, improving the local knowledge base and increasing the level of development and innovation and urged countries to focus their resources and strategies on building and improving institutions (e.g., property rights, size and role of government and regulatory conditions to new venture formation) that could best support drivers of development such as technology-based ventures and enterprises that pursue distinctive business strategies and seek to become fully integrated into a global marketplace.

High-Growth Entrepreneurship

Audretsch prepared a report on "High-Growth Entrepreneurship" for the OECD that was presented in Copenhagen in March 2012.[16] Audretsch examined several important research questions including what constitutes a "high-growth firm"; how prevalent are high-growth firms; what is the economic impact of high-growth firms; and what are the determinants of high-growth firms (e.g., firm-specific or locational)? Based on his findings, Audrestsch noted the importance of promoting entrepreneurship

---

2010 on "Opening Up Innovation: Strategy, Organization and Technology." Imperial College London Business School.

[15] Acs, Z., and L. Szerb. 2010. "The Global Entrepreneurship and Development Index (GEDI)." Paper Presented at Summer Conference 2010 on "Opening Up Innovation: Strategy, Organization and Technology." Imperial College London Business School.

[16] The discussion in this section is adapted from Audretsch, D. 2012. "High-Growth Entrepreneurship." *OECD,* a slide presentation that includes references to the supplementary research referred to in the text. See also Audretsch, D. 2012. *Determinants of High-Growth Entrepreneurship Report Prepared for the OECD/DBA International Workshop on High-Growth Firms: Local Policies and Local Determinants.* Copenhagen.

capital and access to finance and reducing heavy regulatory burdens that make it difficult for new companies to enter the market and increase competitive pressures on incumbents through application of entrepreneurial principles and strategies.

Definition of High-growth Firms

As to what constitutes a "high-growth firm," Audretsch offered several definitions. For example, the 2007 OECD-Eurostat Manual on Business Demography Statistics defined the term to include:

> All enterprises with average annualized growth greater than 20 percent per annum, over a three-year period, and with 10 or more employees at the beginning of the observation period. Growth is thus measured by the number of employees and by turnover.

The same source explained "gazelle firms" to be "[a]ll enterprises up to five years old with average annualized growth greater than 20 percent per annum over a three-year period, and with 10 or more employees at the beginning of the observation period."

Prevalence of High-Growth Firms

Empirical information from the US, UK, and other OECD countries indicated that the high-growth firms were relatively scarce: less than 5 percent of the firms in the US in a 1994 study; between 2 to 4 percent of the firms in the UK in a 2008 study; and less than one percentage of enterprises and less than 2 percent of turnover in most OECD countries according to a 2007 survey. However, the economic impact of the firms was impressive and substantial. A 1994 study covering the US from 1988 to 1992 found that 70 percent of all new jobs in the US during that period created by existing firms, rather than new startups, could be traced to just 4 percent of the firms. Those same 4 percent accounted for 60 percent of all the new jobs created in the US economy during that period. Studies in the UK and for the entire OECD confirmed that between just 2 percent to 4 percent of firms accounted for substantial shares of the growth in employment during any given period.

Determinants of High-Growth

Audretsch explored various theoretic frameworks regarding the determinants of high-growth among firms and described how those frameworks stood up against empirical evidence. Some follow Gilbrat's Law, which holds that firm growth is unpredictable, randomly distributed and not specific to firm or locational characteristics. In contrast, the framework of knowledge spillover theory of entrepreneurship assumes that knowledge created in one organizational context but not fully commercialized will eventually trigger entrepreneurial startups and that entrepreneurship thus provides a conduit for knowledge spillovers from creator organizations to commercialization organizations. Basic assumptions and predictions flowing from this framework are that high growth should be systematically related to high knowledge contexts (firm and locational specific); negatively related to firm age (firm specific) and negatively related to firm size (firm specific).

Sutton and Caves, writing in the *Journal of Economic Literature* in 1997 and 1998 respectively, found that Gibrat's Law did appear to hold for the largest firms and that high-growth opportunities among those firms were not systematically related to firm-specific characteristics such as size and age. However, when the groups of firms was expanded to a broader distribution of firms sizes, they found that growth rates were higher for younger enterprises, growth rates were higher for small enterprises and growth rates were even higher for young and small firms engaged in knowledge-intensive industries. Writing about firm-specific determinants, Henrekson and Johansson said:

> net employment growth rather is generated by a few rapidly growing firms—so-called gazelles—that are not necessarily small and young. Gazelles are found to be outstanding job creators. They create all or a large share of net new jobs. On average, gazelles are younger and smaller than other firms, but it is young age more than small size that is associated with rapid growth.[17]

---

[17] Henrekson, M., and D. Johansson. 2010. "Gazelles as Job Creators—A Survey and Interpretation of the Evidence." *Small Business Economics*, 1.

However, Acs, Parsons, and Tracy reached different conclusions based on data collected about US firms active from 1994 to 2006.[18] They found that while most high impact firms are small, large high-impact firms accounted for most of the new job creation. In addition, they observed that high-impact firms were not young (i.e., the typical high-impact firm was not a startup) and, in fact, the mean age of such firms was 25 years old and they typically had survived startup and adolescent phases prior to being classified as high impact. They also found that high-impact firms could be found in most sectors of the economy, not just in knowledge-intensive industries.

Researchers have explored other characteristics beyond firm size and age to identify reliable determinants of potential for high-growth entrepreneurship. Studies in the UK have found results that support the following propositions:

- Entrepreneurs and management teams of high-growth firms have higher skill levels and educational attainment.
- High-growth firms are more likely to hold intellectual property assets, including trademarks.
- High-growth firms had superior access to finance, particularly access to venture capital financing.
- High-growth firms demonstrated a cultural context promoting high growth and thrived with "high social capital" (i.e., networks, partnerships, relationships, and linkages to other firms and institutions in the form of supply chains and formal strategic alliances).

Researchers examining characteristics of the entrepreneurs and other founders behind high-growth firms found the following to be prevalent: high levels of human capital (education); experience as an entrepreneur and/or as an employee in a high-growth firm; and high levels of industry experience. Notable characteristics of the founding teams of high-growth

---

[18] Acs, Z., W. Parsons, and S. Tracy. 2008. *High-Impact Firms: Gazelles Revisited* (Unpublished manuscript prepared for the United States Small Business Administration).

firms included the size of the founding team, stability of the team members, the time that the members had spent together as a team, heterogeneity of backgrounds and cohesiveness.

As noted above, firms were better able to achieve high-growth status if they were able to gain access to "high social capital" and researchers have focused a lot of effort on "innovation clusters" (i.e., clusters or agglomeration of complementary economic activity and supporting institutions) and their influence on generating higher growth rates for entrepreneurial startups within a cluster. Gilbert et al. and Lechner and Dowling found empirical evidence identifying higher growth rates for entrepreneurial startups within a cluster and others found geographic proximity facilitates accessing and absorbing localized knowledge spillovers.[19] For example, worker mobility was higher in clusters, as was the number of entrepreneurial startups, and clusters had strong localized networks, linkages, and social capital. However, Acs, Parsons, and Tracy argued that high-impact firms are not confined to cluster and could be found in almost every US location. While location with close geographic proximity to an urban area had been important at one time, the importance of urban areas had been decreasing over time and Acs, Parson, and Tracy argued that there was no discernable difference in spatial location of high- and low-impact firms.

Are You a Scale-Up Entrepreneur?

One of the fundamental conditions for growth-oriented entrepreneurship is the desire of the entrepreneurs who are the members of the founding team to not only launch and navigate their businesses to the point of survival but to go beyond that to enjoy significant growth in revenues, employment, and market impact. Isenberg and others have argued that the skills necessary to get through the start-up phase, while obviously crucial, are not the same as those that entrepreneurs need to "scale-up" the business to the point where growth engines are mobilized. Isenberg developed a simple set of assessment questions that entrepreneurs

---

[19] Gilbert, B., P. Anitra, P. McDougall, and D. Audretsch. 2008. "Clusters, Knowledge Spillovers and New Venture Performance: An Empirical Examination." *Journal of Business Venturing* 23, no. 4, p. 405; Gilbert, B., P. McDougall, and D. Audretsch. 2006. "New Venture Growth: A Review and Extension." *Journal of Management* 32, no. 6, p. 926; and Lechner, C., and M. Dowling. 2003. "Firm Networks: External Relationships as Sources for the Growth and Competitiveness of Entrepreneurial Firms." *Entrepreneurship and Regional Development* 15, no. 1, pp. 1–26.

could peruse to determine whether they were "cut out to be a scale-up entrepreneur." These questions were based on interviews that Isenberg conducted with scale-up entrepreneurs from around the world and suggest that backgrounds and actions associated with success in moving through the risky launch stage of a new business to the point where scaling is feasible. Specifically, entrepreneurs should make a note of whether they "agree" or "disagree" with the following statements:

- Something inside compels me to make something that will impact the marketplace.
- I am great at selling things to people that they may not know they want, nor think they have the money to buy.
- I have people on my team who are better than me in several areas of knowledge or practice.
- My venture already has the procedures, policies, and processes in place to be 10 times the size we are today.
- When I don't know what my next step is, I have experienced people I can turn to for ideas.
- There is money out there to fuel a venture that is growing fast; I just have to find it when I am ready.
- When I achieve my objectives I keep raising the bar higher and higher.
- I am one of the best sales people I know.
- Think big; thinking small is a crime.
- I know entrepreneurs just like me who have grown big, fast.
- The sales process is just starting when the customer first says no.
- If my venture stands in one place too long, it runs the risk of perishing. We have to keep moving forward.
- I know how to find great people to hire.
- Nothing gives me a bigger rush than closing a big sale.
- It is more important to know of a big problem that customers have and then look for a solution, than it is to have a solution that is looking for important problems to solve.
- I used to think our great technology would take us to leadership in our market—now I realize it is our team, our organization, our marketing, and our ambition to sell.
- Even though I am a startup, I think more like a market leader than a small business.

The greater the number of times that one "agreed" with a statement, the more likely that he or she had the motivation to scale up their new venture. Two important themes were emphasized when compiling the questions: persistence and experience in all aspects of selling (e.g., sales organization, compensation, pipeline management, and selling skills) and attitude, particularly the ambition to grow the business and a vision for the business that is grand and large.

While sales is one of the most important skills for a scale-up entrepreneurs, others areas for which founding teams might seek out training including personal leadership, effective communication, project management, managing performance, selecting a winning team, negotiation, and managing change.

Sources: Isenberg, D. March 24, 2013. "Find Out If You're a Scale-up Entrepreneur with this Two-Minute Test," Harvard Business Review. See also Isenberg, D. July 2013. Worthless, Impossible, and Stupid: How Contrarian Entrepreneurs Create and Capture Extraordinary Value. Cambridge, MA: Harvard Business Press. Suggestions for training program for scale-up entrepreneurs are available from the "School for Scale-Up offered through the Cambridge Network."

Global Surveys of Growth-Oriented Entrepreneurs and High-Growth SMEs

A report prepared and distributed by The Association of Chartered Certified Accountants in July 2012 titled "High-growth SMEs: understanding the leaders of the recovery" relied on data collected and analyzed by Delta Economics.[20] Delta surveyed "growth oriented" entrepreneurs in BRICSA countries (Brazil, Russia, India, China, and South Africa), in the US and in Europe (i.e., the UK, France, Germany, Italy, Spain, Belgium, and the Netherlands) between October 2010 and December 2011. In deciding which entrepreneurs should be categorized as "growth oriented," Delta limited its survey to entrepreneurs running relatively young businesses (between 2 and 10 years old) that had turned over a minimum of $300,000 after the second year of trading. The chosen companies had already demonstrated extraordinary tenacity and resilience by surviving several years of economic and financial turbulence in the years leading up to the survey, thus making them particularly good candidates for becoming sustaining manager-owned businesses in the future.

Interesting findings from the study included the following[21]:

- The Chinese growth-oriented businesses were the biggest, with an average turnover of $4.13 million (in the last full year of trading) and a median growth rate of 453 percent since start up. Growth rates from start ups in Brazil and India were 311 percent and 216 percent, respectively, the growth rate in the US was 130 percent, the growth rate in the UK was 176 percent and the growth rates among the European countries ranged from 100 percent to 150 percent.
- Average employment among all the businesses was around 25 people and expectations were that employment would

---

[20] The Association of Chartered Certified Accountants, High-growth SMEs: understanding the leaders of the recovery (July 2012) (based on data and analysis provided by Delta Economics in "Challenges and Opportunities for Growth and Sustainability").

[21] Adapted from "Executive Summary" and "Introduction" of report. Id. at pp. 1–8.

nearly double within three years. German GOEs employed an average of 13 people and are expected to employ 21 in three years' time, showing the highest figures in Europe. Employment growth in BRICSA was impressive; GOEs in China employed 32 people at the time of the survey and that number was predicted to increase to 84 in three year's time (comparable numbers for India were 27 and 50).

- The average age of growth-oriented entrepreneurs is 45. The lowest average age was in China at 35: Belgium had the highest average age at nearly 52. China had the largest number of female entrepreneurs at 26 percent and the survey average for female participation was 16 percent.

- 60 percent and 80 percent of initial finance for the surveyed businesses came from self-investment and most of this self-funding (75 percent on average) came from savings. When external financing was used to start a new business, 10 to 25 percent came from family, friends, and "other investors." Once the businesses were launched, few of the entrepreneurs reported problems accessing financing and those were looking for new financing (20 percent) were most interested in growth finance.

- Growth-oriented entrepreneurs in Europe and the US were more likely to seek professional advice during the start-up stage than entrepreneurs in the BRICSA and entrepreneurs in India (62 percent) and China (65 percent) were twice as likely as their counterparts in Europe to turn to family members for advice. Advice from support networks and governmental agencies was disfavored, perhaps because they had little value to offer to growth-oriented businesses.

- Challenges experienced across all of the countries included recruiting people with the right skills and training, accessing government grants and contracts, and overcoming tax and other regulatory hurdles.

- The majority of the businesses showed some level of innovation in the way in which they approached their markets, product differentiation, or research and development

(R&D). Brazilian (55 percent), Chinese (71 percent), and South African (47 percent) companies are more likely to have invested in R&D than their counterparts in the US (41 percent) and Germany (22 percent); however, innovation spending could not be directly related to growth in turnover, perhaps due to length of time that needed to pass before the fruits of investment could be seen in the form of increased revenue growth.

- Internationally-oriented businesses grew faster than domestic only businesses. 60 percent of businesses in the UK and Europe were international, BRICSA entrepreneurs were just under 50 percent international and only 40 percent of US businesses were international. UK sample showed that the international businesses that established as "domestic only" first grew even faster.

- The top four drivers in motivating the entrepreneurs world-wide were in order: following a dream; taking advantage of a market opportunity; getting autonomy over the entrepreneur's time; and "making a lot of money."

International Surveys of "New, Dynamic Ventures"

Llisterri and Garcia-Alba analyzed the results of studies of entrepreneurship conducted by the Inter-American Development Bank that began with surveys of approximately 2,000 nascent and new entrepreneurs in seven countries from Latin America and four from Asia in 2001 and 2002 and expanded in 2005 to include two European countries.[22] The surveys focused on "new, dynamic ventures," which were defined as "firms

---

[22] Llisterri, J., and J. Garcia-Alba. 2008. *HGSMEs in Latin American Emerging Economies*. The paper was prepared for "The OECD Kansas City Workshop," Session III. "From Invention to the Market Place: Acquiring knowledge and intellectual assets: The interaction between large firms and small business in the fast growth process." The surveys were described in Kantis, H., M. Ishida and M. Komori. 2002. *Entrepreneurship in Emerging Economies: The Creation and Development of New Firms in Latin America and East Asia* and Kantis, H. (Editor) with P. Angelelli, and V. Koenig. 2005. *Developing Entrepreneurship: Experience in*

between three and 10 years old that had grown to employ at least 15 workers, and no more than 100, during the study." The results achieved by these companies were compared to a control group of less dynamic SMEs (i.e., new firms that had grown to less than 10 employees during the study). Llisterri and Garcia-Alba provided the following highlights of the profile of the dynamic enterprises, including contrasts to the less dynamic firms:

- The dynamic companies employed an average of 26 workers, and had average annual sales of around $800,000, in their third year in business (average sales per employee for the companies was around $30,000 in the third year).
- In most cases, the projected initial investment amount for the new enterprise was relatively small—$100,000 during the first year; however, most of the companies were successfully launched for less than that amount and only one in five of the companies exceeded that amount.
- Early sales activities of the dynamic firms contrasted sharply to those of the less dynamic firms: first-year sales of the dynamic firms averaged between five and six times the sales of less dynamic firms; the proportion of projects of at least $100,000 was double; and the average team size among the dynamic firms was almost 30 percent larger than the less dynamic firms. The dynamic firms were also much more likely to engage in export activities, although the domestic market was the main source of business for all surveyed firms during their early years.
- A little more than half of the dynamic companies relied on offering differentiated products or services, focusing primarily on their domestic market, and relatively few elected to compete primarily on price as opposed to some form of real innovation. Main customers were other Latin American

Latin America and Worldwide Inter-American Development Bank/Fundes International. Washington, DC: Inter-American Development Bank.

businesses; however, only one in four firms were involved in outsourcing arrangements for their customers.

- Most of the dynamic companies were formed and operated in metropolitan areas and most of them were involved in production and distribution activities (e.g., food, furniture, clothing, metal, mechanic, and metallurgy). One in three of the dynamic companies operated in knowledge-based sectors, primarily software companies providing Internet and telecommunications services.

Llisterri and Garcia-Alba also noted the following personal and professional characteristics of the entrepreneurs who created the dynamic companies:

- Most of the companies were launched by teams of two or more founders.
- Half of the founders came from homes where the father worked independently as a businessman, a professional, or was self-employed.
- Founders typically brought experience from working for another company in a similar sector (i.e., supplier or customer) or being involved in a line of business related to that of the new company. The proportion of the founders who had worked in small, medium, or large firms was relatively similar.
- The average age of the founders was 36–37 and the range was between 31 and 45; however, the average age that the founders started thinking about forming their new business was around 26.
- Main reasons given by the founders for launching their new businesses were the desire for personal fulfillment, the opportunity to apply one's knowledge, and the motivation to improve their personal income.

Llisterri and Garcia-Alba noted that there did not appear to be significant differences in the educational background of the founders of the dynamic and less dynamic companies. In most cases, they had attained high education levels and their college degrees had provided them with important technical knowledge, especially for the dynamic entrepreneurs; however, the educational system did little to transfer other skills necessary for successful entrepreneurship. Dynamic entrepreneurs appeared to have distinctly different learning processes for entrepreneurship than their counterparts among the less dynamic companies. For example, the previous work experiences of dynamic entrepreneurs provided significant advantages in terms of gathering information on business ideas and learning the skills necessary to commercialize those ideas. In addition, dynamic entrepreneurs were better able to establish and mine networks of relationships that provided them with valuable support on such things as identifying business opportunities, accessing funds, forging relationships with executives at larger companies, and obtaining access to information and non-financial resources such as raw materials or facilities. Finally, while self-funding was the financing strategy used by most of the entrepreneurs, the dynamic entrepreneurs appeared to be more adroit at using other financial resources and thus were better position to avoid the constraints on growth associated with satisfying requirements for accessing bank financing.

Growth-Oriented Small Enterprises in Tunisia

Mansouri defined growth-oriented small enterprises in Tunisia as small and medium enterprises in industry and services sectors with a total investment of less than $2.1 million equivalent and which are run directly by their owners who directly and personally assume responsibility for all financial, technical, and moral matters relating to the venture. The number of employees working these ventures range from 10 to 100.[23] Mansouri noted that growth involves job creation, internationalization, product and process innovation, and organizational innovation and growth-oriented companies are focused on improving their competitiveness, increasing

---

[23] Mansouri, F. February 2011. "Challenges in Accessing Finance for Growth-Oriented Small and Micro Entrepreneurs in Tunisia." Presentation for 5th Meeting of MENA-OECD Working Group on SME Policy, Entrepreneurship and Human Capital Development, Casablanca Morroco.

their size, searching for new market opportunities, and acquiring comparing advantages. Factors and firm-specific characteristics relating to growth include the age and size of the firm, internal finance, capital structure, growth opportunities, factor productivity, and the entrepreneur's personal attitude regarding risk.

Qualitative Assessments of High Impact Small Businesses

While most of the research described above has been grounded in quantitative analysis of growth-oriented entrepreneurs and their firms, there has been an explosion of books, reports, and articles providing largely qualitative assessments of high impact small businesses. Consultancies in the human resources field have been especially interested in identifying firms that provide their employees with a health workplace environment. For example, "Great Place to Work" surveyed more than 88,000 employees at 450 small and medium-size businesses in the US to determine which of those businesses should be among the best employers.[24] Among the small companies—defined as companies with 25–249 employees—the firms included on the "top 25" ranged in workforce size from 25 (Squaremouth, St. Petersburg, FL, with $4.5 million in annual revenue) to 235 (Ruby Receptionists, Portland Oregon, with $15.3 million in annual revenue) employees. Annual revenues among the companies in the "top 25" ranged from $3 million (Mammoth HR, Portland, OR, with 40 employees) to $183 million (Granite Properties, Plano, TX, with 150 employees). Revenue per employee among the "top 25" companies ranged from $65,000 (Ruby Receptionists, Portland, OR, with 235 employees and $15.3 million in annual revenue) to $1,89 million (Radio Flyer, Chicago, IL, with 58 employees, $110 million in annual revenues and the Number One ranking among the companies listed in terms of quality of the workplace).

A team of researchers led by Burlingham searched for US companies that had opportunities to grow, and grow quickly, yet decided that while growth was a sign of health it was better to focus on "other, non-financial

[24] *Fortune.* November 1, 2015. "50 Best Small and Medium-Size Companies to Work For." p. 40.

priorities as well, such as being great at what they do, creating great places to work, providing great service to customers, making great contributions to their communities and finding great ways to lead lives."[25] The criteria used for selection was the same as Burlingham had previously used in writing a book called *Small Giants* and included the following:

- The company has been acknowledged as outstanding by those who know the industry best.
- It has had the opportunity to grow much faster, but its leaders decided to focus on being great rather than being just big.
- It has been recognized for its contributions to its community and to society.
- It has maintained its financial health for at least 10 years by having a sound business model, a strong balance sheet, and steady profit margins.
- It is privately owned and closely held.
- It is human-scale, meaning frontline employees have real interaction with top leaders.
- It has "mojo," the business equivalent of charisma, which means that people want to be connected to it as a customer, a supplier, or an employee.

Companies on the list ranged from relatively small in terms of number of employees and annual revenues—Askinosie Chocolate, a Springfield MO chocolate maker with 17 employees and $1.8 million in annual revenue—to much larger businesses such as Abt Electronics, a family-owned, single-location electronics and appliance retailer in Chicago with $400 million in annual revenue and 1,400 employees.12 of the 20 companies on the list had fewer than 250 employees and the annual revenues among the companies in that group ranged from $1.8 million to $110 million (the toymaker Radio Flyer from Chicago, the same company ranked Number One among small companies by Great Places to Work in the survey described above).

[25] Burlingham, B. February 8, 2016. "Best Small Companies." *Forbes*, p. 86.

Case Study: Radio Flyer and Integrated Project Management

Two companies appeared on both of the lists described in the text: Radio Flyer, a Chicago-based toymaker that has been manufacturing popular and iconic toy wagons since 1917; and Integrated Project Management (IPM), a pioneer in the project management sector launched in 1988 and headquartered in Burr Ridge, IL. While the companies are comparable in terms of number of employees [Radio Flyer (101) and IPM (145)], Radio Flyer's annual revenue of $110 million was significantly larger than the $29 million booked by IPM.

The lists were accompanied by very brief descriptions of each of the companies and no specific empirical information about how the companies were operated and managed was presented; however, some general insights were provided about why and how these companies fared so well in the overall surveys:

- The leadership of Radio Flyer, a family-owned business for several generations, had a true passion for the company's product and preserving and enhancing the company's brand. For his part, the founder and CEO of IPM began the business in 1988 with the specific mission of building a company that would last for 100 years.
- Radio Flyer's traditional product line, which was heavily dependent on a single model of toy wagon, was critically assessed and investments were made in new product development to address competition and diversify the revenue stream.
- Input from all Radio Flyer employees, including customer service representatives and administrative assistants, was solicited on all new product designs. As a result, Radio Flyer's employees were highly vested in the success of new product launches. Employees felt like a family and were eager to find ways to improve the products and the way the company worked.
- Radio Flyer's costs were reduced through the use of foreign manufacturers overseen by a company office established in the country (China) where the manufacturing occurred.
- A rigorous hiring process was implemented at Radio Flyer that called for each candidate to complete a writing assignment that included a description of three successes and one failure and a list of 15 questions they wanted to ask about the company. The CEO personally interviewed each candidate before a hiring decision is made.
- Consistent with his goal of "building to last," the first person the founder of IPM hired was someone who could succeed him if he was no longer able to lead the business, and that person remained second in command over 25 years after the company was started.
- IPM focused on implementing "state-of-the-art" management disciplines from the very beginning that included all of the employees (e.g., all full time-employees are actively in the annual planning process). IPM employees also have opportunities for earning "development fees" for bringing in a new client equal to 3 percent of the first year's revenue from the client.
- The founder and CEO of IPM invested time and effort in becoming a pioneer of the fledgling industry—project management—in which the company operated.

Sources: Fortune. November 1, 2015. "50 Best Small and Medium-Size Companies to Work For." p. 40; and Burlingham, B. February 8, 2016. "Best Small Companies." Forbes, 86.

CHAPTER 2

Innovation Clusters

Introduction

Entrepreneurship has become a popular career path in developed and developing countries, a phenomenon that has contributed to the intense interest in the subject shown by researchers and policymakers around the world.[1] In 2011, for example, the Global Entrepreneurship Monitor (GEM), a partnership between the London Business School and Babson College that administers a comprehensive research program to produce annual assessments of national levels of entrepreneurial activity, estimated that there were 388 million entrepreneurs distributed around the globe and engaging starting and running new businesses. Many commentators, beginning with Schumpeter, have argued that entrepreneurship is crucial for understanding economic development.[2] Acs and Virgill noted that "[t]he empirical evidence is ... strong in support of a link between entrepreneurship and economic growth" and that "[s]tudies have found that regional differences in economic growth are correlated to levels of entrepreneurship.[3]

---

[1] Interestingly, studies of entrepreneurial behavior around the world have concluded that "entrepreneurs think alike, no matter what country they call home" (*The Wall Street Journal*, February 6, 1992, p. AI. See also Berger B. 1991. *The Culture of Entrepreneurship*. San Francisco: The Institute for Contemporary Studies.

[2] Acs, Z., and L. Szerb. June 2010. "The Global Entrepreneurship and Development Index (GEDI)." Paper Presented at Summer Conference 2010 on "Opening Up Innovation: Strategy, Organization and Technology," Imperial College London Business School. A review of the literature regarding the relationship of entrepreneurship to economic development appeared in Acs, Z., and N. Virgill. 2009. "Entrepreneurship in Developing Countries." *Foundations and Trends in Entrepreneurship*.

[3] Acs, Z., and N. Virgill. 2009. "Entrepreneurship in Developing Countries." Jena Economic Research Papers, No. 2009–023.

Shane et al. were particularly interested in improving the quality and conciseness of research on how human motivations influence entrepreneurship; however, they suggested a model that may well have broader application in the design of an analytical framework for studying the various factors that influence entrepreneurship.[4] Shane et al. believed that entrepreneurship was best viewed as a "process" that occurred over an extended period of time, rather than an isolated event or moment in time when a person decide whether he or she should become an "entrepreneur." This process included a number of stages, including recognition of opportunities, development of ideas about how to pursue the opportunity by turning it into new products or services and, finally, execution of the activities required to harvest the desired profits from the opportunities. The execution phase involved array of tasks and activities such as evaluating the feasibility of the opportunity, product/service development, assembly of human and financial resources, organizational design and "market making" (i.e., identification and pursuit of customers). In their model, the success or failure of the entire entrepreneurial process, and the decisions made along the way, are influenced by several important factors. The motivational traits of the prospective entrepreneur is one of them; however, in order to get a complete picture it is necessary to also take into account other factors that Shane et al. felt had been ignored by previous researchers such as cognitive factors, the nature of the opportunity, and environmental conditions.[5]

Institutional Environment and Entrepreneurship

Several scholars have argued that the rate of new venture formation and growth is directly influenced by the institutional environment, both

---

[4] Shane, S., E. Locke, and C. Collins. 2003. "Entrepreneurial Motivation." *Human Resource Management Review* 13, pp. 257–79, 274–76.

[5] Id. at p. 258 ("In our arguments, we explicitly assume that all human action is the result of both motivational and cognitive factors, the latter including ability, intelligence and skills. We also assume that entrepreneurship is not solely the result of human action; external factors also play a role . . .").

formal and informal, in which the venture is operating.[6] New ventures, being both new and small, must struggle to gain legitimacy and survive in their external environment and one way to do that is to conform to the norms and practices that have been prescribed and sanctioned by the institutional environment. In many ways, the institutional environment limits the range of strategic options that are available to new ventures in a society[7] and thus plays an important role in both the creation and destruction of entrepreneurial activities in that society.[8] It is, therefore, not surprising that one area of comparative research with respect to international entrepreneurship is comparing the institutional environment of different societies as to their favorability for entrepreneurship. The need for this type of research is particularly compelling for emerging economies as they struggle to identify and implement policies that can promote economic development including policies to encourage entrepreneurs to form new ventures that hopefully create new jobs and contribute to an increase in overall economic welfare.[9] In fact, several researchers have

---

[6] Eunni, R. 2010. "Institutional Environments for Entrepreneurship in Emerging Economies: Brazil vs. Mexico." *World Journal of Management* 2, no. 1, pp. 1–18 (citing Hwang, H., and W. Powell. 2005. "Institutions and Entrepreneurship." In *Handbook of Entrepreneurship Research*, 179–210, eds. Z. Acs and D. Audretsch. Norwell, MA: Kluwer; Gnyawali, D., and D. Fogel. 1994. "Environments for Entrepreneurship Development: Key Dimensions and Research Implications." *Entrepreneurship Theory and Practice* 18, no. 4, pp. 43–62; and Aldrich, H. 1990. "Using an Ecological Perspective to Study Organizational Founding Rates." *Entrepreneurship Theory and Practice* 14, no. 3, pp. 7–24).

[7] Ahlstrom, D., and G. Bruton. 2002. "An Institutional Perspective on the Role of Culture in Shaping Strategic Actions by Technology-Focused Entrepreneurial Firms in China." *Entrepreneurship Theory and Practice* 26, no. 4, pp. 53–70; and Roy, W. 1997. *Socializing Capital: The Rise of the Large Industrial Corporation in America*. Princeton, NJ: Princeton University Press.

[8] Aldrich, H., and G. Wiedenmayer. 1993. "From Traits to Rates: An Ecological Perspective on Organizational Foundings." In *Advances in Entrepreneurship, Firm Emergence, and Growth*, 145–95, eds. J. Katz and A. Brockhaus. Greenwich, CT: JAI Press.

[9] Wennekers, A., and A. Thurik. 1999. "Linking Entrepreneurship and Economic Growth." *Small Business Economics* 13, no. 1, pp. 27–55; and Baumol, W. 2002. *The Free Market Innovation Machine: Analyzing the Growth Miracle of*

asserted that the rate and trajectory of entrepreneurial activities in emerging countries is significantly influenced by the institutional environment in those countries.[10]

While North defined the "institutional framework" of a society as "the fundamental political, social and legal ground rules, which establish the basis for production and distribution,"[11] Scott laid the foundation for meaningful comparison by suggesting that the formal and informal institutions that influence business can be categorized as follows: regulatory institutions, which include the formal system of laws and regulations which have been adopted and enforced in a given community, society, or country; normative institutions, which include the commercial standards and conventions that have been established and recognized through professional and trade associations in a given community, society, or country; and cognitive institutions, which encompass the culture-specific beliefs regarding socially appropriate behavior which are acquired by persons

---

Capitalism. Princeton, NJ: Princeton University Press (both observing that new venture creation leads to the creation of new jobs and economic welfare).

[10] Peng, M., and P. Heath. 1996. "The Growth of the Firm in planned Economies in Transformation: Institutions, Organizations and Strategic Choice." *Academy of Management Review* 21, pp. 492–528; Ahlstrom, D., and G. Bruton. 2002. "An Institutional Perspective on the Role of Culture in Shaping Strategic Actions by Technology-Focused Entrepreneurial Firms in China." *Entrepreneurship Theory and Practice* 26, no. 4, pp. 53–70; Smallbone, D., and F. Welter. 2001. "The Distinctiveness of Entrepreneurship in Transition Economies." *Small Business Economics* 16, no. 4, pp. 249–62; Smallbone, D., and F. Welter. 2006. "Conceptualizing Entrepreneurship in a Transition Context." *International Journal of Entrepreneurship and Small Business* 3, no. 2, pp. 190–206.

[11] North, D. 1990. *Institutions, Institutional Change, and Economic Performance.* New York, NY: Norton. In a later work, North commented that institutions "form the incentive structure of a society, and the political and economic institutions, in consequence, are the underlying determinants of economic performance" and then defined institutions as "the humanly devised constraints that structure human interaction . . . [t]hey are made up of formal constraints (such as rules, laws, constitutions), informal constraints (such as norms of behavior, conventions, self-imposed codes of conduct), and their enforcement characteristics." North, D. 1994. "Economic Performance Through Time." *American Economic Review* 84, no. 3, pp. 359–68, 360.

as they undergo the socialization process in the community, society or country.[12]

Global Entrepreneurship Monitor

The GEM is a partnership between the London Business School and Babson College that administers a comprehensive research program to produce annual assessments of national levels of entrepreneurial activity. The project was first launched in 1999, when it covered just 10 countries, and has since grown to cover as many as 85 countries in subsequent years and is recognized as the largest ongoing study of entrepreneurial dynamics in the world. The main objectives of the GEM program are measurement of differences in the level of entrepreneurial activity between countries, uncovering the factors that lead to appropriate levels of entrepreneurship and making suggestions for policies that may lead to enhancement of national levels of entrepreneurial activity. The GEM, like other models, has always been focused on exploration of the link between entrepreneurship and economic development and its original model attempted to integrate several variables thought necessary to enable business activity including entrepreneurial capacity, entrepreneurial opportunities, and certain "entrepreneurial framework conditions" discussed in more detail below. Recently, the GEM model was revised to take into account that the contribution of entrepreneurs to an economy varies according to its phase of economic development, with those phases being defined in the

---

[12] Scott, W. 1995. *Institutions and Organizations*. Thousand Oaks, CA: Sage. Scott's Classification Model has been adopted by a number of other researchers. See, for example, Ahlstrom, D., and G. Bruton. 2002. "An Institutional Perspective on the Role of Culture in Shaping Strategic Actions by Technology-Focused Entrepreneurial Firms in China." *Entrepreneurship Theory and Practice* 26, no. 4, pp. 53–70; Kostova, T. 1997. "Country Institutional Profiles: Concept and Measurement." *Academy of Management Best Paper Proceedings*, pp. 180–89; Parkhe. A. 2003. "Institutional Environments, Institutional Change and International Alliances." *Journal of International Management* 9, pp. 305–16; and Bruton, G., V. Fried, and S. Manigart. 2005. "Institutional Influences on the Worldwide Expansion of Venture Capital." *Entrepreneurship Theory and Practice* 29, no. 6, pp. 737–60.

manner suggested by Porter et al. and described elsewhere in this chapter, namely "factor-driven economies," "efficiency-driven economies," and "innovation-driven economies." A large amount of information regarding the work of the GEM researchers is available at its website and in addition to the annual global reports, such as the one for 2011 referred to herein, there are a number of country-specific "national reports" that provide international benchmarking, local context, and recommendations for national entrepreneurship policies.

The GEM is based on a conceptual model of the institutional environment and its effect on entrepreneurship. The model recognizes the importance of the social, cultural, and political context in which entrepreneurial activities occur and assumes that these contextual factors influence three sets of conditions: basic requirements, which include institutions, infrastructure, macroeconomic stability, health, and primary education; "efficiency enhancers," which include higher education, goods and labor market efficiency, financial market sophistication, technological readiness and market size; and the "entrepreneurial framework conditions" discussed below. Entrepreneurship itself is measured by looking at the entrepreneurship profile of prospective and actual entrepreneurs, including their attitudes, activities, and aspirations; and at the entrepreneurship process itself. The GEM researchers acknowledge that entrepreneurship is a process that extends over multiple phases, thus allowing opportunities for assessing the state of entrepreneurship in a particular society at different phases.

The adult population surveys provide a means for measuring individual involvement in venture creation, identifying the motives of entrepreneurs, measuring the aspirations of entrepreneurs with respect to pursuing high growth and/or activities in foreign markets and understanding the societal climate for entrepreneurship. The "climate for entrepreneurship" includes not only the perceptions of prospective entrepreneurs regarding the availability of opportunities around them, their ability to start businesses and the value of doing so but also the availability of positive support from others regarding entrepreneurship as measured by "societal perceptions" of entrepreneurship and the willingness of vendors and investors to supply tangible and financial resources. The national expert surveys measure the following nine EFCs:

- **Finance**: The availability of financial resources—equity and debt—for small and medium enterprises (SMEs) (including grants and subsidies);
- **Government policies**: The extent to which taxes or regulations are either size-neutral or encourage SMEs;
- **Government programs**: The presence and quality of direct programs to assist new and growing firms at all levels of government (national, regional, and municipal);
- **Entrepreneurial education and training**: The extent to which training in creating or managing SMEs is incorporated within the education and training system at all levels (primary, secondary, and post-school);
- **R&D transfer**: The extent to which national research and development will lead to new commercial opportunities and is available to SMEs;
- **Commercial and professional infrastructure**: The presence of property rights and commercial, accounting, and other legal services and institutions that support or promote SMEs;
- **Entry regulation**: Contains two components including "Market Dynamics," which is the level of change in markets from year to year, and "Market Openness," which is the extent to which new firms are free to enter existing markets;
- **Physical infrastructure and services**: Ease of access to physical resources—communication, utilities, transportation, land or space—at a price that does not discriminate against SMEs; and
- **Cultural and social norms**: The extent to which social and cultural norms encourage or allow actions leading to new business methods or activities that can potentially increase personal wealth and income.

Busenitz et al. "Country Institutional Profiles"

As discussed above, Scott suggested that the formal and informal institutions that influence business could be placed into three categories—regulatory, normative, and cognitive—and these categories served as the basis for the creation of a survey instrument by Busenitz et al. that has often been used as a means for measuring a country's institutional profile.[13] The survey items for the various categories, sometimes referred to as "dimensions," included the following:

- Regulatory: The level of government assistance and special support to individuals looking to start their own business; the degree to which the government sets aside contracts for new and small businesses; the level of government sponsorship of organizations that assist in the development of new businesses; and the degree to which the government assist entrepreneurs who have failed in earlier business to start new businesses.

- Cognitive: The knowledge and skills possessed by people in the country pertaining to establishing and operating a new business as indicated by the degree to which individuals know how to legally protect a new business; the degree to which entrepreneurs know how to cope with high levels of risk and manage those risks; and the availability of information regarding markets for products and services to be offered by new businesses.

- Normative: The degree to which entrepreneurship is an admired career path within the society; the degree to which innovative and creative thinking is valued and viewed as a route to success within the society; and the degree to which entrepreneurs are admired in the society.[14]

---

[13] Busenitz, L., C. Gomez, and J. Spencer. 2000. "Country Institutional Profiles: Unlocking Entrepreneurial Phenomena." *Academy of Management Journal* 43, no. 5, pp. 994–1003. For more on Scott's classification model, see Scott, W. 1995. *Institutions and Organizations.* Thousand Oaks, CA: Sage.

[14] It should be noted, however, that when discussing the normative dimension a comparison of the institutional environment for entrepreneurship in Mexico and Brazil, Eunni included the role of industry and trade associations, formalization of recordkeeping and accounting requirements, the sophistication of local banking and insurance industries, support for new business incubation, and the availability of funding for the promotion of innovation. Eunni, R. 2010. "Institutional

Kantis' Entrepreneurial Development System

Kantis suggested a model of an "entrepreneurial development system" created by adding in a combination of elements and factors that have an impact, both positive and negative, on the process and, ultimately, on the efficient development of entrepreneurs and entrepreneurial firms. Kantis grouped these factors into a short list of categories, which he introduced and described as follows[15]:

- *Social and economic conditions* reflect the profile of the households from which potential entrepreneurs emerge and take into factors such as the degree of social fragmentation, access to education, flow of information relevant to entrepreneurial activity, income levels and overall macroeconomic conditions such as the behavior of demand or the degree of economic stability;
- *Societal culture*, which is discussed extensively in this publication, influences the formation of the "entrepreneurial spirit" and cultural values impact important factors such as the social value ascribed to the entrepreneur and attitudes toward the risk of failure;
- *Productive structure and dynamism* refers to the sector and regional profile and the size of the existing enterprises and institutions and is considered important because it determines the type of work and professional experience, including

---

Environments for Entrepreneurship in Emerging Economies: Brazil vs. Mexico." *World Journal of Management* 2, no. 1, pp. 1–18.

[15] The summary description of each of the categories is based on Kantis, H. 2005. "A Systematic Approach to Enterprise Creation." In *Developing Entrepreneurship: Experience in Latin America and Worldwide*, ed. H. Kantis, 17–27, 20–22. Washington, DC: Inter-American Development Bank. Kantis deployed his model as a tool for cross-border comparison of entrepreneurial activities and policies. For further discussion, see "Factors Influencing Entrepreneurial Activities" in "Entrepreneurship: A Library of Resources for Sustainable Entrepreneurs" prepared and distributed by the Sustainable Entrepreneurship Project (www.seproject.org).

opportunities for development of entrepreneurial skills and
networks of relationships (see below), which individuals can
obtain prior to becoming entrepreneurs;

- *Personal aspects,* which refers to socio-demographic profile of
  the entrepreneur—which are influenced by his or her family,
  educational and work environments—and his or her entrepreneurial skills (e.g., propensity to assume risk, tolerance for
  hard work, managerial capacities, and creativity);

- *Networks,* which include the assistance provided through his
  or her social networks (i.e., friends and family), institutional
  networks (i.e., business associations, institutions of higher
  learning, and/or development agencies) and commercial
  networks (i.e., suppliers and customers);

- *Factor markets,* which provide entrepreneurs with access to
  financial resources (e.g., bank loans, venture capital, and/or
  government financing), skilled labor and professional services
  (accountants, consultants, etc.) and suppliers of inputs and
  equipment; and

- *Regulations and policies* that have an impact on enterprise
  creation, such as taxes, procedural requirements for formally
  establishing a new firm and initiatives and programs to
  develop entrepreneurship.

Global Entrepreneurship and Development Index

Acs and Szerb believed that the GEM project and its focus on the business
formation process in a large number of countries, while impressive and
valuable, fell short due to its failure to incorporate the different impacts
of new businesses and its ranking of countries based primarily on the
number of new businesses without regard to their success from a financial
perspective or in terms of job creation, improving the local knowledge
base and increasing the level of development and innovation.[16] Specifically, they were critical of the tendency of empirical investigations of

---

[16] Acs, Z., and L. Szerb. June 2010. "The Global Entrepreneurship and Development Index (GEDI)." Paper Presented at Summer Conference 2010 on

entrepreneurship to take "simple, one-dimensional approaches" even as modern research theories implicitly acknowledged that entrepreneurship required a multi-dimensional definition.[17] For example, they argued that indexes such as GEM's TEA that are based solely or primarily on measures of "self-employment," business ownership, new business creation, or the percentage of the adult population willing to engage in "entrepreneurial" activity[18] neglected important differences in the "quality" of entrepreneurial activity (e.g., skills, innovation, and high growth); differences in environmental factors; and the efficiency and level of the society's institutional setup (e.g., property rights, size and role of government, and regulatory conditions to new venture formation).

In a report prepared for the US Small Business Administration Acs and Szerb explained that the GEDI captures the contextual features of

---

"Opening Up Innovation: Strategy, Organization and Technology." Imperial College London Business School.

[17] Id.

[18] With regard to self-employment, see Acs, Z., D. Audretsch, and D. Evans. 1994. "Why does the Self-Employment Rates Across Countries and Over Time?" CERP Working Paper No. 871. Center for Economic Policy Research; Blanchflower, D., A. Oswald, and A. Stutzer. 2001. "Latent Entrepreneurship Across Nations." *European Economic Review* 45, nos. 4–6, pp. 680–91; and Grilo, I., and R. Thurik. 2008. "Determinants of Entrepreneurship in Europe and the US." *Industrial and Corporate Change* 17, no. 6, pp. 1113–45. With regard to business ownership rate, see Carree, M., A. van Stel, R. Thurik, and S. Wennekers. 2002. "Economic Development and Business Ownership: An Analysis Using Data of 23 OECD Countries in the Period 1976–1996." *Small Business Economics* 19, no. 3, pp. 271–90; and Cooper, A., and W. Dunkelberg. 1986. "Entrepreneurship and Paths to Business Ownership." *Strategic Management Journal* 7, no. 1, pp. 53–68. With regard to new venture creation, see Gartner, W. 1985. "A Conceptual Framework for Describing the Phenomenon of New Venture Creation." *The Academy of Management Review* 10, no. 4, pp. 696–706; and Reynolds, P., D. Storey, and P. Westhead. 1994. "Cross-national Comparisons of the Variation in New Firm Formation Rates." *Regional Studies* 28, no. 4, pp. 443–56. For information on the TEA, see Acs, Z., P. Arenius, M. Hay, and M. Minniti. 2005. *Global Entrepreneurship Monitor: 2004 Executive Report*. Babson Park, MA: Babson College and London: London Business School; and Bosma, N., K. Jones, E. Autio, and J. Levie. 2008. *GEM Executive Report 2007*. Babson College, London Business School, and Global Entrepreneurship Research Consortium.

entrepreneurship by focusing on three broad areas referenced in their definition of "entrepreneurship" referred to above:

> The first is entrepreneurial attitudes, a society's basic attitudes toward entrepreneurship through education and social stability. The second area of focus is entrepreneurial activity, what individuals are actually doing to improve the quality of human resources and technological efficiency. The final area is entrepreneurial aspirations, how much of the entrepreneurial activity is being directed toward innovation, high-impact entrepreneurship, and globalization.[19]

The GEDI created by Acs and Laszlo was a "super-index" based on societal scores on three sub-indexes measuring activity, aspiration, and attitudes[20]:

- The entrepreneurial attitude sub-index, or "ATT," focuses on identifying and measuring "entrepreneurial attitudes" associated with a society's entrepreneurship-related behavior. Among the areas of interest with respect to ATT are the potential for perceiving novel business opportunities, "fear of failure," "startup skills," and personal networks. Acs and Laszlo believed that several institutional factors would influence ATT including the size of the market, education, business risk, Internet usage, and culture.

---

[19] Acs. Z., and L. Szerb. 2010. *Global Entrepreneurship and the United States.* Washington, DC: US Small Business Administration Office of Advocacy. http://sba.gov/content/global-entrepreneurship-and-united-states (accessed April 30, 2011).

[20] Acs, Z., and L. Szerb. June 2010. "The Global Entrepreneurship and Development Index (GEDI)." Paper Presented at Summer Conference 2010 on "Opening Up Innovation: Strategy, Organization and Technology," Imperial College London Business School. The article includes an extensive discussion of the methodology used in compiling and weighting the indexes and a description of the institutional variables used in the indexes.

- The entrepreneurial activity sub-index, or "ACT," makes the GEDI distinguishable from other empirical measures of entrepreneurship through its focus on measuring "high growth potential start-up activity." Among the factors taken into account are "opportunity start-up motives," sophistication or intensity of technology involved, level of education, and product/service uniqueness. Acs and Laszlo believed that the relevant institutional factors relating to ACT included ease of doing business (referred to as "business freedom"), the availability and absorption of the latest technology, and the level of human development (i.e., education and training).

- The entrepreneurial aspiration sub-index, or "ASP," relates to what Acs and Laszlo called "the distinctive, qualitative, strategy related nature of entrepreneurial activity" and incorporates "the efforts of the early-stage entrepreneur to introduce new products and services, develop new production processes, penetrate foreign markets, substantially increase the number of firm employees, and finance the business with either formal or informal venture capital, or both."[21]

Acs and Szerb concluded that public policy makers must takes steps to strengthen institutions before a country's entrepreneurial resources can be fully deployed.[22] Thus, for example, steps must be taken to increase "business freedom" by easing restrictions on the ability of entrepreneurs to start, operate, and close a business and making governmental processes with respect to business approvals more efficient and transparent.

---

[21] Acs, Z., and E. Autio. 2011. "The Global Entrepreneurship and Development Index: A Brief Explanation." www.imperial.ac.uk/business-school (accessed April 30, 2011). One of the institutional variables used by Acs and Szerb was "business strategy" and referred to "the ability of companies to pursue distinctive strategies, which involves differentiated positioning and innovative means of production and service delivery." See Acs, Z., and L. Szerb. June 2010. "The Global Entrepreneurship and Development Index (GEDI)." Paper Presented at Summer Conference 2010 on "Opening Up Innovation: Strategy, Organization and Technology," Imperial College London Business School.

[22] Id.

In addition, the government must take appropriate action to improve the society's human capital, through education and training to increase the capacity to absorb and apply new technologies, and reduce corruption and business risk by creating a legal framework that provides investors with a higher level of trust in entering into business transactions. Institutional building should also be targeted toward activities that have been identified as drivers of development such as technology-based ventures and enterprises that pursue distinctive business strategies and seek to become fully integrated into a global marketplace.

Innovation Clusters

Many believe that the first serious reference to geographic concentrations of interconnected companies—"clusters"—appeared in the work of Cambridge economist Alfred Marshall, who described "industrial districts" that arose from an observed tendency of specialized companies to cluster together to form geographic concentrations of expertise and economic activity.[23] Marshall viewed these tendencies positively and, in fact, wrote in 1890 about how "…great are the advantages which people following the same skilled trade get from near neighboring to one another…."[24] Other economists built on Marshall's initial theory by suggesting and adding other "necessary elements" for the creation and maintenance of "innovation clusters" including the importance of a "self-interested economic agents," or "entrepreneurs," willing to take on and attempt to overcome the risks associated with unproven technologies to seek substantial profits. According to Schumpeter, these entrepreneurs drove the process of transferring and transforming emergent technologies into new products, services, and product models and creating new methods for organizing economic activities to establish new industries and markets.[25]

---

[23] Lazzeretti, L., S. Sedita, and A. Caloffi. 2014. "Founders and Disseminators of Cluster Research." *Journal of Economic Geography* 14, no. 1, p. 21.

[24] Dearlove, D. July 1, 2001. "The Cluster Effect: Can Europe Clone Silicon Valley?" *Strategy+Business.* citing Marshall, A. 1890. *Principles of Economics.*

[25] For extensive discussion of Schumpeter's theories relating to "entrepreneurship," see Schumpeter, J. 1949. *Theory of Economic Development.*

Romer suggested that technological progress is driven by researchers searching for new ideas for innovations which can eventually provide them with monopoly profits.[26]

A century after Marshall's work Porter undertook an extension examination and analysis of business clusters and uncovered evidence of a strong positive relationship between the proximity of specialized companies and extraordinary competitive success.[27] Dearlove provided the following description of how Porter painted the boundaries of clusters:

> Professor Porter suggests that clusters encompass an array of linked industries and other entities important to competition, including suppliers of specialized inputs and providers of specialized infrastructure. Clusters also extend downstream to channels and customers and laterally to manufacturers of complementary products, and to companies in industries with common skills, technologies, or inputs. Clusters often include governmental and other institutions, such as universities, standard-setting agencies, and think tanks, as well as providers of specialized training, education, information, research, and technical support.[28]

Porter famously observed that the importance of clustering contrasts dramatically with the idea that the emerging global economy is breaking down barriers and making location less important as a condition for becoming a "global player" and referred to what he called the "paradox of location": "Paradoxically, the enduring competitive advantages in a global

---

[26] See Romer, D. 2011. "Endogenous Growth." In *Advanced Macroeconomics*, 4th ed. 101.

[27] Porter explained his research and theories in a number of articles including Porter, M. 1998. "Clusters and the New Economics of Competition." *Harvard Business Review* 76, no. 6, p. 77; and Porter, M. 2000. "Location, Competition, and Economic Development: Local Clusters in a Global Economy." *Economic Development Quarterly* 14, no. 1, p. 16.

[28] Dearlove, D. 2001. "The Cluster Effect: Can Europe Clone Silicon Valley?" *Strategy+Business*.

economy lie increasingly in local things—knowledge, relationships, and motivation that distant rivals cannot match."[29]

The following sections provide a selective, and far from complete, overview of some of the research and commentary on the necessary elements of an innovation cluster. Work in this area is important as it informs and drives the strategies that countries, regions, and cities take in order to attract and retain growth-oriented entrepreneurs who can make significant contributions to the community through job creation and rising income levels for residents. The suggestions are varied; however, there seems to be general consensus about the importance of elements such as accessible domestic markets, including access to small and large companies and governments as customers; human capital, including managerial and technical talent and experience in launching and building knowledge-intensive firms; funding and finance; support systems, including mentors/advisors, professional services, incubators/accelerators and a network of entrepreneurial peers; regulatory framework and infrastructure; education and training; major universities as catalysts; and cultural support.[30]

On a practical level, innovation clusters should be able to provide entrepreneurs with the resources and tools they need to launch their emerging companies, including networks that can be used to tap into the human resources necessary to build a founding team and recruit knowledge workers who can create and develop new products and services; professional investors (e.g., venture capitalists) and/or corporate partners with the capital necessary to support the product development activities of the founders and the expansion of the company to the point required for effective promotion and distribution of the product or service; professional and business advisors, including attorneys, accountants, bankers, insurance brokers, and consultants; regulatory framework that facilitates

---

[29] Id. Citing Porter, M. 2000. "Location, Competition, and Economic Development: Local Clusters in a Global Economy." *Economic Development Quarterly* 14, no. 1, p. 16.

[30] Entrepreneurial Ecosystems around the Globe and Company Growth Dynamics: Report Summary for the Annual Meeting of the New Champions 2013 (World Economic Forum, September 2013).

creation of business entities and establishment of governance systems and allows entrepreneurs to create and protect an intellectual property rights portfolio; and strategic partners that can collaborate with the new firm as suppliers, customers, manufacturers, distributors, and research and development partners.[31]

Milken Institute's Elements for Creation of "High-Tech Clusters"

In 2000, The Milken Institute published the results of its study of the clustering phenomenon that included a list of eight key elements in the creation of high-tech clusters: the presence of cutting-edge research facilities and top educational institutions, which the Institute argued was probably the most important factor in the incubation of high-tech industries; a close network of research institutions, entrepreneurs, and risk-tolerant venture capitalists to facilitate rapid adoption of emerging technologies; a trained and educated work force; technology spillovers from nearby high-tech industries; the availability of venture capital; high quality of place, such as a pleasant climate, low crime rate, and good schools; a reasonable cost of living, especially affordable housing; and factors that favorably affect the cost of doing business, such as low land prices.[32]

"Golden Triangle"

Pfeifer et al. argued that the level and intensity of innovation in a specific geographic area (i.e., an "innovation cluster") was a function of the linkages among learning centers, the public sector, and the private sector on

---

[31] For further discussion of the specific issues and challenges associated with launching an emerging company, as well as a description of the characteristics of such a firm, see the Part on "Launching a New Business." In "Entrepreneurship: A Library of Resources for Sustainable Entrepreneurs" prepared and distributed by the Sustainable Entrepreneurship Project (www.seproject.org).

[32] Dearlove, D. July 1, 2001. "The Cluster Effect: Can Europe Clone Silicon Valley?" *Strategy+Business* (citing The Milken Institute, Blueprint for a High-Tech Cluster: The Case of the Microsystems Industry in the Southwest (2000)).

technology innovation, a so-called "Golden Triangle."[33] They defined a "learning center" as including the local "academic or non-corporate institutions that conduct research and build knowledge assets and intellectual capital, and serve as a source of technology innovation" and noted that it was important to analyze not only the connections between learning centers and the public and private sectors but also the connections between different learning centers in the area. The "public sector" was defined as "the national, regional, or local policies, bodies and regulations that contribute to or constrain the development of technology innovation" and included the relevant organizations and institutions, national and local laws and regulations, fiscal policies, research and development funding, and infrastructure support. Finally, Pfeifer et al. defined the "private sector" as including the companies "that seek to apply research for commercial benefit."

Pfeifer et al. who were particularly interested in understanding and comparing the innovation environments found in Silicon Fen in the United Kingdom and Campinas in Brazil, suggested the following list of assessment criteria that could be used to measure and test linkages between the three points of their Golden Triangle:

- Building of knowledge assets: Examination of the roles played by business, academic, and the government communities in establishing and supporting the means to grow and retain knowledge capital and assets generated within the region.
- Accessibility of financial capital: Accessibility of financial capital within the vicinity (e.g., venture capital in the region, nearby financial services centers, government loans and grants, direct foreign investment).

---

[33] The discussion of the Golden Triangle model, including the list of the specific assessment tools, is adapted from Pfeifer, A., I. Alalawi, L. Heim, O. Pound, D. Pressman, and S. Tsang. 2009. *The Golden Triangle: A Comparative Perspective—Silicon Fen (UK) and Campinas (Brazil)*. See also Whittaker, D., ed. 2009. *Comparative Entrepreneurship: The UK, Japan and the Shadow of Silicon Valley*. Oxford: Oxford University Press.

- Intellectual property laws: The local laws and regulations relating to the protection of intellectual property, e.g., copyrights, patents, and other restraints such as ownership of intellectual property between universities and the researchers.
- Mechanism for commercialization: The local channels for taking products or ideas to the markets and the support and mechanism in creating spin-off companies.
- Public policies on innovation: The national or regional policies on innovation, funding schemes, educational or human resources policies, government focus on regional innovation clusters.
- Fiscal environment and policies: The national and local taxation regulation on tax breaks for certain fostering innovations, investment incentives (e.g., credit/discount on land purchase, requirements for foreign investment, deposits within local areas for the first few years, likelihood of taxation policy to ensure regional efficient spending).
- Supporting infrastructure: Local information, communication, transport, housing infrastructure for supporting the local workforce in building knowledge capital.

Entrepreneurial Ecosystems

In recent years it has become increasingly popular to refer to innovation clusters as "entrepreneurial ecosystems," a concept that Mason and Brown discussed in 2013 as part of the broader question of what types of policy initiatives should be taken to promote the creation and maturation of high growth firms (HGFs).[34] Mason and Brown cited the works of several researchers that supported the premise that HGFs have a significant impact on economic development. For example, the OECD and Brown

---

[34] Mason, C., and R. Brown. November 7, 2013. "Entrepreneurial Ecosystems and Growth Oriented Entrepreneurship." International Workshop on Entrepreneurial Ecosystems and Growth Oriented Entrepreneurship Organized by OECD LEED Programme and Dutch Ministry of Economic Affairs Workshop; Background Paper (Final Version: January 2014).

et al. have reported that HGFs drive productivity growth, create new employment, increase innovation, and promote business internationalization,[35] and Henrekson and Johansson, after conducting a meta-analysis of prior empirical studies, concluded that "a few rapidly growing firms generate a disproportionately large share of all net new jobs compared with non-high growth firms. This is a clear-cut result ... [T]his is particularly pronounced in recessions when Gazelles continue to grow."[36] Others have suggested that HGFs have important spill-over effects that are beneficial to the growth of other firms in the same locality and industrial cluster.[37]

Mason and Brown noted that recognition of the disproportionate value of HGFs to economic development has led policymakers to consider adopting support programs for high growth entrepreneurship that are more "systems-based" and which rely mainly on "relational" forms of support including building connections and networks among entrepreneurs, prioritizing development of "blockbuster entrepreneurs" with significant economic potential and institutional alignment of priorities.

---

[35] Organization for Economic Co-operation and Development. 2013. *An International Benchmarking Analysis of Public Programmes for High-Growth Firms (OECD LEED) programme*. Paris; and Brown, R., C. Mason, and S. Mawson. 2014. *Increasing the Vital 6%: Designing Effective Public Policy to Support High Growth Firms*. London: National Endowment for Science Technology & Arts (NESTA).

[36] Henrekson, M., and D. Johansson. 2010. "Gazelles as Job Creators: A Survey and Interpretation of the Evidence." *Small Business Economics* 35, no. 2, pp. 227–44, 240.

[37] Mason, G., K. Bishop, and C. Robinson. 2009. *Business Growth and Innovation; The Wider Impact of Rapidly Growing Firms in UK City-Regions*. London: NESTA. http://niesr.ac.uk/pdf/ 190509_94959.pdf; Du, J., Y. Gong, and Y. Temouri. 2013. *High Growth Firms and Productivity: Evidence from the UK*. London: NESTA. http://nesta.org.uk/publications/working_papers/assets/features/high_growth_ firms_and_productivity; Feldman, M., J. Francis, and J. Bercovitz. 2005. "Creating a Cluster While Building a Firm: Entrepreneurs and the Formation of Industrial Clusters." *Regional Studies* 39, pp. 129–41; and Brown, R. 2011. "The Determinants of High Growth Entrepreneurship in the Scottish Food and Drink Cluster." In *The Handbook of Research on Entrepreneurship in Agriculture and Rural Development*. eds. G. Alsos, S. Carter, and E. Ljunggren, and F. Welter. Cheltenham: Edward Elgar.

A number of researchers have referred to the overall framework for providing this type of support as an "entrepreneurial ecosystem,"[38] which
Mason and Brown defined, based on their own synthesis of definitions
throughout the relevant literature, as:

> a set of interconnected entrepreneurial actors (both potential
> and existing), entrepreneurial organizations (e.g., firms, venture
> capitalists, business angels, and banks), institutions (universities,
> public sector agencies, and financial bodies) and entrepreneurial
> processes (e.g., the business birth rate, numbers of HGFs, levels of
> "blockbuster entrepreneurship," number of serial entrepreneurs,
> degree of sell-out mentality within firms and levels of entrepre-
> neurial ambition) which formally and informally coalesce to
> connect, mediate and govern the performance within the local
> entrepreneurial environment.[39]

While Mason and Brown added that entrepreneurial ecosystems were
geographically bounded, they noted that cities did not have to be a particular size to qualify and pointed to Austin, Texas and Boulder, Colorado
in the US and Cambridge in England as examples of smaller cities that
had been successful at developing what they referred to as "thriving entrepreneurial ecosystems." Mason and Brown also explained that a system
could emerge around one industry or evolve and expand to cover several
industries.[40]

---

[38] Zacharakis, A., D. Shepard, and J. Coombs. 2003. "The Development of Ven-
ture-Capital-Backed Internet Companies: An Ecosystem Perspective." *Journal of
Business Venturing* 18, no. 2, p. 217; Napier, G., and C. Hansen. 2011. *Ecosystems
for Young Scaleable Firms*. FORA Group; and Feld, B. 2012. *Startup Communities: Building an Entrepreneurial Ecosystem in Your City*. Hoboken, NJ: Wiley.
[39] Mason, C., and R. Brown. 2013. "Entrepreneurial Ecosystems and Growth
Oriented Entrepreneurship." International Workshop on Entrepreneurial Ecosystems and Growth Oriented Entrepreneurship. Organized by OECD LEED
Programme and Dutch Ministry of Economic Affairs Workshop; Background
Paper (Final Version: January 2014), 5.
[40] Id. at pp. 5–6.

For researchers like Isenberg, an entrepreneurial ecosystem is a "strategy for economic development" that depends on several key factors or domains: a conducive culture, enabling policies and leadership, availability of appropriate finance, quality human capital, venture friendly markets for products, and a range of institutional supports.[41] For their part, Mason and Brown argued that the distinguishing features of entrepreneurial ecosystems include

> a core of large established businesses, including some that have been entrepreneur-led (entrepreneurial blockbusters); entrepreneurial recycling—whereby successful cashed out entrepreneurs reinvest their time, money and expertise in supporting new entrepreneurial activity; and an information-rich environment in which this information is both accessible and shared.[42]

Mason and Brown also believed that in order for entrepreneurial ecosystems to thrive there must be a group of "dealmakers" who are involved in a fiduciary capacity in several entrepreneurial ventures, ready availability of start-up and growth capital, and a supportive community of large firms, universities, and service providers.[43]

As for the specific steps that should be taken to launch and stimulate entrepreneurial ecosystems, Mason and Brown argued that policymakers would need to focus on several dimensions including direct support of entrepreneurial actors through accelerators and incubators; development of entrepreneurial organizations and resource providers such as business angels, venture capital, banks, service providers, universities; creation of connectors within the ecosystem through public-private partnerships and alliances and peer-to-peer learning; and development and nurturing of

---

[41] Isenberg, D. 2011. *The Entrepreneurship Ecosystem Strategy as a New Paradigm for Economy Policy: Principles for Cultivating Entrepreneurship*, 4. Babson Park, MA: Babson Entrepreneurship Ecosystem Project, Babson College.

[42] Mason, C., and R. Brown. November 7, 2013. "Entrepreneurial Ecosystems and Growth Oriented Entrepreneurship." International Workshop on Entrepreneurial Ecosystems and Growth Oriented Entrepreneurship Organized by OECD LEED Programme and Dutch Ministry of Economic Affairs Workshop; Background Paper (Final Version: January 2014), 1.

[43] Id.

an entrepreneurial environment or culture within the ecosystem through entrepreneurship education, role models, peer-to-peer networking, and entrepreneurial recycling.[44] Mason and Brown noted while there was a role for governments to play in developing entrepreneurial ecosystems, they should limit their involvement to facilitation and leave the details to the private sector, experienced local entrepreneurs and/or leading local companies. Key to success would be the ability to create a local culture that was favorable to startup activity and which promoted and accepted entrepreneurial risk-taking. Experienced entrepreneurs could do their part by training, coaching, and mentoring their prospective peers and local companies could contribute by allowing and encouraging spinoff of promising ideas into new firms. In many cases it will be necessary to provide training to both local entrepreneurs and investors on the financing process until such time as the ecosystem has a community of experienced angel and venture capital investors.

Research on Entrepreneurial Ecosystems and Growth-Oriented Entrepreneurship

An extensive collection of materials relating to entrepreneurial ecosystems and growth-oriented entrepreneurship were developed and made available for distribution as part of a workshop on the topic organized by the OECD LEED Programme and the Netherlands' Ministry of Economic Affairs. The workshop covered three important topics. First, presenters looked into how entrepreneurial ecosystems could be defined, how they work, whether they have primarily a national or local dimension, and what their main drivers of success or failures are. The second topic focused on the actors needed for an entrepreneurial ecosystem to be growth-oriented. Prominent and important actors include not only investors, established firms, serial entrepreneurs, knowledge institutions, and service providers, but also "connectors" or "dealmakers" that serve as the glue keeping the entrepreneurial ecosystem together (e.g., science parks, industry associations, entrepreneurs' clubs, and entrepreneur mentors). The third topic was the role of policy for growth-oriented entrepreneurship and the specific measures that can and should be taken by national and local governments. Important links to papers and other presentations from the workshop, can be found here: http://oecd.org/cfe/leed/entrepreneurialecosystemsandgrowth-orientedentrepreneurshipworkshop-netherlands.htm

---

[44] Mason, C., and R. Brown. November 7, 2013. "Entrepreneurial Ecosystems and Growth Oriented Entrepreneurship." International Workshop on Entrepreneurial Ecosystems and Growth Oriented Entrepreneurship Organized by OECD LEED Programme and Dutch Ministry of Economic Affairs Workshop; Summary Report.

Entrepreneurial Ecosystems in Europe

While the area surrounding Cambridge University in the UK has long been considered to be among the world's innovation clusters, policymakers throughout Europe have long been concerned about development of entrepreneurial ecosystems to keep pace with rivals in the US and Asia. Dearlove pointed out that Europe does not lack large and important technology companies such as Nokia and Ericsson in Scandinavia; however, these companies have long histories and did not have their roots in technology clusters as their competitors in Silicon Valley and Route 128 near Boston did. In reality, the clusters that have developed around Europe, including those in the UK, have generally not been able to incubate larger companies and many of the European startups have eventually sold their technology off into the hands of American multinationals that have established subsidiaries in or near the European clusters.[45] In general, small technology companies established in Europe have been unable to bridge the gap between development and commercialization and have often surrendered much of their intellectual property rights to US entrepreneurs with more experience in bringing products to market.

Writing in the early 2000s, Dearlove reported that European technology companies were beginning to adopt alternative business models based on a growing realization that steps needed to be taken to proactively transform the basic building blocks developed during scientific research into commercial products.[46] These alternative models included not only the traditional research activities, but also technology consulting, incubation activities, and licenses of intellectual property to startup companies accompanied by investments to assist those licenses with the hard work of commercialization. As time went by Europe began to develop a new set of recognized technology clusters including the areas around Munich and Stuttgart in Germany; Sophia Antipolis in Southern France; Kista in Stockholm; around Dublin in Ireland; around Oulu in Finland; and in the Etna Valley in Sicily.[47]

---

[45] Dearlove, D. 2001. "The Cluster Effect: Can Europe Clone Silicon Valley?" *Strategy+Business.*

[46] Id.

[47] Id.

According to Choi, it is possible to identify and distinguish two different types of high-tech clusters in Europe.[48] The first, which is best illustrated by Cambridge's Silicon Fen, is the "naturally occurring" cluster that emerges and grows around research universities. The second requires active governmental intervention to launch and accelerate the growth of a cluster and the governmental toolkit typically includes public subsidies of technology companies and the infrastructure in which they are born and grow, creative tax incentives and adoption of laws and regulations intended to ease the business formation process and enhance the ability of entrepreneurs to appropriate the potential profits from their innovations. Sophia Antipolis, which is a large science park located on the French Riviera between Nice and Cannes, and Dublin are both examples of policy-led clusters.

While policy-led clusters have achieved some modest success, in general they have fallen well short of initial expectations. According to Dearlove, Cohan described the view of critics of this approach as follows: "The basic problem with the cluster concept for policy-makers is that it implicitly assumes that regional economic strength can be mandated by government."[49] Cohan went on to argue:

> The reality is that regional economic powerhouses became strong because entrepreneurs and research universities spawned new companies. Supporting industries, such as venture capital, law, accounting, and IPO underwriting, emerged to meet the needs of the entrepreneurs. The role of government in these geographic regions was primarily to stay out of the way of the entrepreneurs and to provide some incentives in the form of lower capital gains taxes. In regions where governments try to mandate entrepreneurial behavior they fail.[50]

---

[48] Id.

[49] Id. (citing Cohan, P. 1999. *Net Profit*).

[50] Dearlove, D. 2001. "The Cluster Effect: Can Europe Clone Silicon Valley?" *Strategy+Business* (citing Cohan, P. 1999. *Net Profit*). Dearlove also cited a February 2001 report by the Department of Trade and Industry that identified 154 regional business clusters then operating in the UK and concluded, following extensive analysis, that new clusters cannot be kick-started by public policy

Surveying and Measuring Entrepreneurship and Innovation

Suggesting and measuring factors generally associated with innovative capacity has become a popular pastime in academia and business publications. The GEM mentioned above was one of the first, and highly ambitious, efforts in this area and has been followed by a wide range of rankings and analyses of entrepreneurship, innovation, and competitiveness.

Global Entrepreneurship Monitor

As mentioned above, GEM is a partnership between the London Business School and Babson College that administers a comprehensive research program to produce annual assessments of national levels of entrepreneurial activity. The project was first launched in 1999, when it covered just 10 countries, and has since grown to cover as many as 85 countries in subsequent years and is recognized as the largest ongoing study of entrepreneurial dynamics in the world. The main objectives of the GEM program are measurement of differences in the level of entrepreneurial activity between countries, uncovering the factors that lead to appropriate levels of entrepreneurship and making suggestions for policies that may lead to enhancement of national levels of entrepreneurial activity.

The GEM researchers measure "total early-stage entrepreneurial activity," or "TEA," for each country by identifying and combining entrepreneurs who are either engaged in nascent activities or acting as new business owners. In addition to a TEA rate for each country, the GEM researchers also score and rank countries with respect to established business ownership rate, discontinuation of businesses, necessity-driven entrepreneurship as a percentage of TEA, and improvement-driven opportunity entrepreneurship as a percentage of TEA. Countries are grouped by their phase of economic development so that comparisons can be made among comparable countries and researchers can also track

---

initiatives. Porter also discussed the role of government in clustering extensively in Porter, M. 2000. "Location, Competition, and Economic Development: Local Clusters in a Global Economy." *Economic Development Quarterly* 14, no. 1, p. 16.

how entrepreneurial activities change as countries develop economically and socially. As noted above, the GEM researchers borrowed from Porter by suggesting that countries go through three stages of economic development: a factor-driven stage; an efficiency-driven stage; and, finally, an innovation-driven stage.[51] Acs and Szerb have provided the following brief descriptions of each of these stages:[52]

The factor-driven stage is marked by high rates of agricultural self-employment and countries in this stage generally compete based on low-cost efficiencies in the production of commodities or low value-added products. Countries in this stage do not create knowledge that can be used for innovation nor do they use knowledge to engage in exporting activities. In the 2011 GEM survey, for example, seven of the 54 countries fell into the factor-driven stage including Guatemala (with the highest TEA among the group) and Pakistan (with the lowest TEA among the group).[53]

The efficiency-driven stage requires that countries engage in efficient productive practices in large markets so that firms can achieve and exploit economies of scale. Industries in this stage are generally manufacturing-based and focused on the production and distribution of basic goods and services. Self-employment tends to decline during this stage and capital, labor, and technology begin to emerge as the key drivers of productivity. In the 2011 GEM survey, for example, 24 of the 54 countries fell into the efficiency-driven stage including China, Chile, and Peru with the highest TEA rates among the group and Hungary, Malaysia, and Russia with the lowest TEA rates among the group.[54]

---

[51] Porter, M. 2002. *Global Competitiveness Report.* Geneva: World Economic Forum.

[52] Acs, Z., and L. Szerb. June 2010. "The Global Entrepreneurship and Development Index (GEDI)." Paper Presented at Summer Conference 2010 on "Opening Up Innovation: Strategy, Organization and Technology," Imperial College London Business School.

[53] Kelley, D., S. Singer, and M. Herrington. 2012. *Global Entrepreneurship Monitor: 2011 Global Report*, 10. Babson Park, MA: Global Entrepreneurship Research Association.

[54] Id. at pp. 10–11.

In the innovation-driven stage, the key input is "knowledge" and decisions about embarking on new projects are based on primarily on expected net returns and the likelihood that economic activities can generate high value added products and services. In the 2011 GEM survey, for example, 23 of the 54 countries fell into the efficiency-driven stage including Australia and the US with the highest TEA rates among the group and Denmark, Japan, and Slovenia with the lowest TEA rates among the group.[55]

As discussed below, as countries transition between stages of development there will be changes in their entrepreneurship profile. Even among comparable countries, countries at the same stage of economic development, the rate and profile of entrepreneurship may vary significantly due to environmental constraints that are specific to a given country. For example, a country may have a high rate of start-up activity but fail to maintain that rate at the established business phase due to societal factors that make it difficult for nascent entrepreneurs to maintain their momentum and get their businesses to the point where they are sustainable. In addition, the GEM researchers have often cautioned that higher TEAs do not necessarily imply better economic conditions. For example, certain nations with higher levels of TEA, such as the United Arab Emirates, Iceland, and Greece, experienced severe economic distress in the early 2010s and some innovation-driven economies, such as Japan, have historically had low levels of TEA.

For 2011 survey results obtained from interviewing over 140,000 adults in 54 countries led the GEM researchers to make the following estimates[56]:

- 388 million entrepreneurs were actively engaged in starting and running new businesses;
- There were 163 million women early-stage entrepreneurs; however, in most of the surveyed countries the entrepreneurship rates for women were significantly lower than for men;

---

[55] Id. at p. 11.
[56] Id. at p. 4.

- There were 165 million young early-stage entrepreneurs (i.e., between the ages of 18 and 35) and, in general, early-stage entrepreneurs tended to be young to mid-career (i.e., from ages 25–44) and entrepreneurs tended to be younger in the efficiency-driven economies;
- 141 million of the early-stage entrepreneurs expected to create at least five new jobs in the next five years;
- 65 million of the early-stage entrepreneurs expected to create 20 or more new jobs in the next five years;
- 69 million of the early-stage entrepreneurs offered innovative products and services that are new to customers and have few other competitors; and
- 18 million of the early-stage entrepreneurs sell at least 25 percent of their products and services internationally.

The results reported by the GEM researchers reflect some of the nuances in their assessment of entrepreneurial activity. In particular, the researchers who prepared the results of the 2011 GEM survey noted the interest in identifying the "profile of entrepreneurs," rather than just the number of entrepreneurs, and that the report focused on three profile factors: inclusiveness, including the availability of entrepreneurial activities to women and people of various ages; industry, realizing that the skills and other attributes of entrepreneurs will differ from industry-to-industry; and, finally, impact, which looks at the role of innovation in an entrepreneurial endeavor and the aspirations of the entrepreneur with respect to internationalization and growth.[57]

The 2011 GEM survey also generated data that allowed the researchers to reach various conclusions regarding entrepreneurial activities in the 54 countries that were part of the survey. Highlights included the following[58]:

With regard to potential entrepreneurship, countries included among the factor-driven economies displayed higher average perceptions about entrepreneurial activities in their area than countries falling into the other

---

[57] Id. at pp. 6, 15–21.
[58] Id. at pp. 7–18.

two development levels and also displayed higher perceived capabilities to start a business than countries classified as efficiency- or innovation-driven economies. The researchers explained that these differences could be attributed to individuals having different ideas about what kind of businesses to establish based on their level of development and noted that consumer-oriented businesses were the most popular in factor-driven economies while innovation-driven economies had a higher proportion of business services enterprises than countries in the other two development levels.

Potential entrepreneurship varied significantly among countries in the same level of economic development. For example, the researchers pointed out that while Bangladesh, a factor-driven economy, scored highly on perceived opportunities the pool of entrepreneurs in that country was reduced by a high lack of confidence in ability to start a business and a high fear of failure. On the other hand, another factor-driven economy, Venezuela, displayed only an average level of perceived opportunities but had strong positive opinions regarding ability to start a business and a low fear of failure.

A number of European countries who had been pummeled by adverse economic conditions at the time of the survey had relatively low perceptions of opportunities and low rates of opportunities and capabilities were also found in some of the innovation-driven Asian economies such as Japan, Korea, and Singapore. The score from the respondents from the US with respect to perceived opportunities fell near the average of the innovation-driven economies; however, they were generally quite confident of their abilities to start a new business and had a relatively low fear of failure.

The researchers asked respondents whether they felt that entrepreneurship was a "good career choice" and found that the percentage of respondents answering affirmatively declined as economic development improved. This finding was supported by the fact that perceptions about the status of entrepreneurs were higher in the factor-driven economies than in the other two development levels.

Entrepreneurial intentions, as measured by the percentages of individuals who had not yet started a business but had expressed an intention to start a business within the next three years, were highest in factor-driven economies. Entrepreneurial intentions declined as the level of development increased. There was evidence that entrepreneurial intentions were influenced by the types of economic activities typically carried out in a country with countries that placed a high emphasis on extractive resources (i.e., Russia and the United Arab Emirates) having relatively low entrepreneurial intention rates.

From 2010 to 2011 there was a significant increase in TEA rates in many economies across all development levels, an interesting trend given the turbulent economic conditions that countries all over the world were experiencing during that time.

Consumer-oriented business (e.g., retail enterprises) tended to dominate entrepreneurial activities at the factor-driven and efficiency-driven stages; however, business services, which rely and compete on knowledge and technology, were the most prominent among entrepreneurs in the innovation-driven economies.[59]

Among factor-driven economies necessity- and improvement-driven opportunism as a percentage of total TEA is roughly the same; however, as the level of development increased the necessity-driven opportunism became less important as a motivator to start a new business and improvement-driven opportunism became more important as a motivator.[60]

Comparing TEA rates to the rate of established business ownership, the GEM researchers found that TEA rates were highest in the factor-driven economies and decreased as the level of development increased and necessity-driven entrepreneurship declined. There were significantly more early-stage entrepreneurs than established business owners in the

---

[59] Id. at p. 18. In addition to consumer-oriented businesses and business services, the GEM survey also tracked extractive and transforming activities.

[60] The GEM defined "necessity-driven" entrepreneurs as those persons who start new businesses because they have no other work options and need a source of income while improvement-driven entrepreneurs are defined as those persons interested in pursuing an opportunity and who do so in order to improve their incomes and/or independence in their work. Id. at p. 13. For further discussion of necessity-driven entrepreneurship and other methods for classifying "types of entrepreneurship," see "Definitions and Types of Entrepreneurship" in "Entrepreneurship: A Library of Resources for Sustainable Entrepreneurs" prepared and distributed by the Sustainable Entrepreneurship Project (www.seproject.org).

factor-driven economies; however, on average, by the time a country reached the innovation-driven stage it could be expected that the TEA rate would drop slightly become the level of established business ownership.

Business discontinuance declined as the level of economic development increased, a finding attributed, at least in part, to the higher proportion of entrepreneurs at the earlier development phases and the higher levels of risk that those entrepreneurs must overcome. Business closings among factor- and efficiency-driven economies were often blamed on a lack of profitability and sources of financing while business discontinuances in the innovation-driven economies were more likely due to retirement, sale, or the desire to pursue another opportunity.

The GEM researchers also focused on three other important measures of entrepreneurship: entrepreneurs' expectations regarding growth in terms of number of persons that will be employed in five years, the degree of "innovation" involved in the entrepreneur's product or service and "internationalization" (i.e., the extent to which entrepreneurs sell to customers in foreign countries).[61] Innovation was measured by looking at the extent to which an entrepreneur's product or service was new to some or all customers of the entrepreneur and whether there were few or no other businesses offering the same product or service. Measured in this way innovation is context-dependent and determined by the entrepreneur's main customer market. Accordingly a product or service offered for the first time in one country would be deemed innovative with respect to that country even if the product or service is commonly sold by number of competitors in other countries. Internationalization was measured by looking at what percentage of the entrepreneurs in a given country had at least 25 percent of their customers in foreign countries.

The survey results included growth expectations for the 54 countries at three levels: 0–4 employees in five years (low growth expectations), 5–19 employees in five years (medium growth expectations), and 20 or more employees in five years (high growth expectations). While factor-driven economies had more entrepreneurs, most of them were in the low growth

---

[61] Kelley, D., S. Singer, and M. Herrington. 2012. *Global Entrepreneurship Monitor: 2011 Global Report*, 18–21. Babson Park, MA: Global Entrepreneurship Research Association.

category. On the other hand, innovation-driven economies had a lower percentage of entrepreneurs but those entrepreneurs were much more likely to have high growth expectations. As for innovativeness, it is not surprising that the researchers found that it increased along with the level of economic development. Finally, internationalization, like innovation, was lowest in the factor-driven economies but rose as economic development improved. Internationalization appeared to be influenced by factors other than just economic development such as the size of the population and land mass in the "home country" and the size and diversity of the local market.

The GEM researchers suggest that the nature of entrepreneurship and its contribution to the national economy changes as economies development and development should be accompanied by changes in emphasis of governmental policies. For example, since economic development in factor-driven economies is largely driven by the "basic requirements" in the GEM conceptual model of the relationship between the institutional context and entrepreneurship, emphasis during that phase should be placed on development of institutions, infrastructure, macroeconomic stability, and health and primary education. Once an economy transitions into the efficiency-driven phase, government policies should be focused "efficiency enhancers" including the proper (i.e., "efficient") functioning of goods and labor markets, development of higher education systems, enhancement of technological readiness, and increasing the scope and sophistication of financial markets. While these initiatives may not have an immediate direct impact on entrepreneurship they will provide the foundation for attracting and enabling higher levels of entrepreneurship in the future. Finally, economies in, or about to enter, the innovation-driven phase requires governmental attention to each of the various EFCs mentioned above in order to create jobs and spur technical innovation.

The highest ratings for EFCs in the 2011 GEM survey came from the experts in the innovation-driven economies, which confirmed the assumption that the basic requirements and efficiency enhancers included the GEM theoretical model are more developed in those economies and thus it is appropriate to focus on the EFCs. Three of the EFCs were also considered to be quite important by experts from the factor-driven economies: post-school entrepreneurship education; internal market dynamics;

and cultural and social norms for entrepreneurship. Significant differences between innovation-driven economies and factor-driven economies
were found with respect to the following EFCs: government programs,
physical infrastructure, R&D transfer, finance, and national policy.[62]

Global Entrepreneurship and Development Index

As mentioned above, Acs and Szerb believed that the GEM project and
its focus on the business formation process in a large number countries,
while impressive and valuable, fell short due to its failure to incorporate
the different impacts of new businesses and its ranking of countries based
primarily on the number of new businesses without regard to their success
from a financial perspective or in terms of job creation, improving the local
knowledge base and increasing the level of development and innovation.[63]
Acs and Szerb, like others,[64] observed that an understanding of entrepreneurship requires going beyond the traits and characteristics of the
individual entrepreneur to also consider institutional variables and they
noted that "[t]he dynamics of the [entrepreneurial] process can be vastly
different depending on the institutional context and level of development within an economy."[65] They explained that entrepreneurship occurs
within an environment that is influenced by economic development and
that development directly impacts and strengthens institutions that eventually affect characteristics that are considered to be vitally important
to the phenomenon of entrepreneurship such as quality of governance,

---

[62] Id. at pp. 22–23.

[63] Acs, Z., and L. Szerb. June 2010. "The Global Entrepreneurship and Development Index (GEDI)." Paper Presented at Summer Conference 2010 on "Opening Up Innovation: Strategy, Organization and Technology," Imperial College
London Business School.

[64] See, for example, Busenitz, L., and J. Spencer. 2000. "Country Institutional
Profiles: Unlocking Entrepreneurial Phenomena." *Academy of Management
Journal* 43, no. 5, pp. 994–1003.

[65] Acs, Z., and L. Szerb. June 2010. "The Global Entrepreneurship and Development Index (GEDI)." Paper Presented at Summer Conference 2010 on "Opening Up Innovation: Strategy, Organization and Technology," Imperial College
London Business School.

access to capital and other resources, the perceptions of entrepreneurs and incentive structures for prospective entrepreneurs. Researchers have found evidence that the strengthening of institutions causes more entrepreneurial activity to be shifted toward "productive entrepreneurship" which, in turn, strengthens economic development.[66] Entrepreneurial activity reaches its highest level of intensity as countries go through the innovation-driven stage and eventually levels off as institutions are fully developed and the country has achieved a high level of innovation.[67]

Acs and Szerb reported the rankings of the 71 countries in their survey and noted that their findings were significantly and highly correlated with other well-known measurement tools such as the Global Entrepreneurship Index, Index of Economic Freedom, and Global Competitiveness Index. When reporting the rankings Acs and Szerb placed the countries into their appropriate stage of development using the aforementioned categories developed by Porter (i.e., factor-driven, efficiency-driven, and innovation-driven).[68] Acs and Szerb pointed out the following notable findings from the 2010 rankings:

- Nordic and Anglo-Saxon countries in the innovation driven stage of development were in the front ranks. Denmark and Sweden led the GEDINDEX, Iceland and Norway joined them in the top ten, and Finland was 13th overall. The US and Canada were third and fourth and Australia, Ireland, and Switzerland also did well although they were weak in at least one of the sub-indexes.
- The most populous EU countries were in the middle part of the rankings, with the United Kingdom at 14th, Germany at 16th, France at 18th, Italy at 27th and Spain at 28th.

---

[66] Acemoglu, D., and S. Johnson. 2005. "Unbundling Institutions." *Journal of Political Economy* 113, no. 5, pp. 949–95.

[67] Fukuyama, F. 1989. "The End of History?" *The National Interest* 16, pp. 3–18.

[68] Further discussion of the views of Acs and Szerb on the contributions of entrepreneurship to development and relative importance of institutional factors in promoting entrepreneurship at different stages of economic development is included elsewhere in this part.

Acs and Szerb suggested that there was a relationship between low levels of entrepreneurship in those countries and their relatively weak economic performance over the decade leading up to the rankings.

- The bottom of the rankings hosted a number of low GDP-level factor-driven countries such as Jamaica, Bosnia-Herzegovina, Venezuela, Brazil, Philippines, Iran, Bolivia, Ecuador, and Uganda.

Entrepreneurial performance of the innovation-driven countries was significantly different from the efficiency-driven countries, with the largest differences observed with respect to indicators of new products, "non-fear of failure," internationalization and risk capital. Factor-driven and efficiency-driven countries were more similar regarding entrepreneurship indicators, but notable differences could be identified with respect to attitudinal indicators of "non-fear of failure" and "cultural support."

Acs and Szerb also used "cluster analysis" to divide the surveyed countries into five country groups that possessed similar entrepreneurial features. The first group included most of the factor-driven economies in the survey with low scores on measures of international connections and development of human resources. A number of the efficiency-driven economies were in the next cluster and Acs and Szerb noted that these economies were involved in trying to increase entrepreneurship from what was currently a relatively low level of development. The remaining three clusters were home to most of the innovation-driven economies and broke down into innovation leaders, such as the US and the Scandinavian countries who topped the list for several reasons including the availability of formal and informal venture finance and excellence in technology application and adaptation; innovation followers that generally took a "follower" approach in identifying and pursuing innovation strategies first launched within the "leader" group; and innovation challengers who possessed some relative advantages that would allow them to compete with the leaders in certain instances. The most significant differences among the three "innovation" clusters could be found in the area of "entrepreneurial attitudes," which included opportunity perception, startup skills, "non-fear of failure," networking, and cultural support.

In general, the innovation leaders were the same countries who led the GEDINDEX rankings; Latin American countries appeared in the factor-driven cluster; and most of the Eastern European and Balkan countries and five out of six of the African countries appeared in the efficiency transformers cluster. An interesting, although not totally surprising, finding was the tremendous diversity among the Asian countries with respect to entrepreneurship. Acs and Szerb observed that the poorer Asian countries fell into the resource- or factor-driven clusters while highly populated Asian countries such as China, India, and Indonesia could be found in the efficiency-driven cluster. Among the richer Asian countries, Hong Kong was an innovation challenger and Japan, Korea, and Singapore were innovation followers. None of the Asian countries appeared in the innovation leader cluster. Acs and Szerb concluded that the cluster analysis provided further confirmation of a strong and positive relationship between economic development and entrepreneurship.

In 2010, the five highest ranking countries on the entrepreneurial attitude sub-index, or "ATT," were, in order, New Zealand, Australia, Canada, Sweden, and Denmark. The US was 6th. The five lowest ranking countries were Guatemala, Indonesia, Russia, Syria, and Uganda. The five highest ranking countries on the entrepreneurial activity sub-index, or "ACT," were, in order, Denmark, Canada, Puerto Rico, Ireland, and Norway. The US was 8th. The five lowest ranking countries were Bosnia and Herzegovina, Morocco, the Philippines, Serbia, and Uganda. The five highest ranking countries on the entrepreneurial aspiration sub-index, or "ASP," were, in order, the US, Iceland, Singapore, Israel, and Sweden. The five lowest ranking countries were Bolivia, Guatemala, Iran, Kazakhstan, and the Philippines. Sub-index scores of a few of the other major global economic players were as follows: China—54th on ATT, 53rd on ACT, 26th on ASP, and 40th overall on GEDI; Japan—47th on ATT, 23rd on ACT, 22nd on ASP, and 29th overall on GEDI; and India—62nd on ATT, 51st on ACT, 40th on ASP, and 53rd overall on GEDI. Not surprisingly, there were several instances of significant deviations, upward and downward, on one of the sub-indexes in relation to the other sub-indexes and overall GEDI. For example, Germany placed 7th on ASP but its ranking of 24th on ATT drove its overall GEDI placement down to 16th. Israel, not surprisingly, was 4th in ASP but its placement as 38th and 21st in ATT and ACT, respectively, led to an overall GEDI for this famously entrepreneurial society of 21st.

Bloomberg Innovation Quotient

One of the most well-known efforts has been Bloomberg's annual rankings of innovation among countries based on the compilation of a Global Innovation Index that featured a Bloomberg Innovation Quotient (BIQ) for each of the ranked countries that incorporated the seven factors which are described below, along with their relative weighting as a percentage[69]:

- "R&D Intensity" was measured by R&D as a percentage of GDP (20 percent)
- "Manufacturing Capability" was measured by looking at manufacturing valued-added as a percentage of GDP and products with high R&D intensity (aerospace, computers, pharmaceuticals, scientific instruments, and electrical machinery) as a percentage of total manufactured exports (20 percent)
- "Productivity" was measured by looking at GDP per employed person (total annual hours worked) (10 percent)
- "High-tech Density" was measured by looking at the number of high-tech public companies (e.g., aerospace and defense, biotechnology, hardware, software, semiconductors, Internet software and services, and renewable energy companies) as a percentage of all publicly listed companies (10 percent)
- "Tertiary Efficiency" was measured by looking at enrollment and graduation ratios in all subjects for post-secondary students; tertiary graduation ratio of students who majored in science, engineering, manufacturing, and construction; and annual new graduates as a percentage of the total workforce (population aged 15–64) (10 percent)

---

[69] Bloomberg Rankings: Global Innovation Index (as of April 20, 2012) (Sources included Bloomberg, World Bank, World Intellectual Property Organization, The Conference Board, OECD and UNESCO).

- "Researcher Concentration" was measured by looking at R&D researchers per one million people (20 percent)
- "Patent Activity" was measured by looking at patents granted as a percentage of applications submitted and application granted worldwide; and resident filings per $1 million of R&D spent (10 percent)

In general the data used was collected over a 10 year period prior to compilation of the scores and rankings and countries had to be ranked for at least five of the 10 years to qualify, which meant for example that the final universe for the 2012 rankings was limited to 81 countries or sovereign regions and that certain countries discussed in detail in this Survey, such as India and Vietnam, were not eligible for inclusion.

The following table summarizes the rankings of various countries as of 2012 with respect to their overall BIQ and each of the seven factors described above (factors rankings for countries outside of the first ten have been limited to factors as to which a country ranked particularly high or low in relation to the other countries):

Country	BIQ	R&D	MAN	PROD	TECH	TE	RC	PAT
Finland	1	3	10	15	7	2	1	21
Singapore	2	12	4	6	9	n/a	5	45
Korea	3	7	5	30	5	1	20	5
Japan	4	4	17	25	11	19	3	6
Sweden	5	2	20	14	2	11	4	18
Germany	6	9	12	16	3	50	15	12
US	7	6	39	3	1	25	6	13
Switzerland	8	5	15	20	14	28	12	31
France	9	11	57	8	8	9	17	14
Austria	10	13	18	9	13	39	18	23
Denmark	14						7	
UK	15			10		10		
Norway	21		62	2			8	
Russia	22		45	47		3		1
Israel	29	1	78		4			50
China	32		3	70		68		

Country	BIQ	R&D	MAN	PROD	TECH	TE	RC	PAT
South Africa	33			50				3
Mexico	46	53				61	50	64
Brazil	57							
Egypt	61							

The following table presents the countries with the highest scores on each of the factors included in the BIQ as of 2012:

One of the anticipated purposes of rankings such as those popularized by Bloomberg is that policymakers will use the information to prioritize steps that should be taken to improve the capacity for innovation in their countries and that changes should be expected as time goes by and countries implement their innovation strategies. In fact, Bloomberg's own rankings for 2014 reflected the following changes from 2012 in the rankings determined by the BIQ[70]:

Country	2012	2014
Finland	1	4
Singapore	2	8
Korea	3	1
Japan	4	2
Sweden	5	7
Germany	6	3
US	7	6
Switzerland	8	16
France	9	9
Austria	10	17
Denmark	14	11
UK	15	10
Norway	21	15
Russia	22	14
Israel	29	5

---

[70] Bloomberg Business Week. January 2015. *What's in the Innovation Sandwich?* 19–25.

	R&D Intensity	Manufacturing Capability	Productivity	Hi-Tech Density	Researcher Concentration	Tertiary Efficiency	Patent Activity
1	Israel	Thailand	Luxembourg	US	Finland	Korea	Russia
2	Sweden	Malaysia	Norway	Sweden	Iceland	Finland	Ukraine
3	Finland	China	US	Germany	Japan	Russia	South Africa
4	Japan	Singapore	Ireland	Israel	Sweden	Australia	Belarus
5	Switzerland	Korea	Belgium	Korea	Singapore	Ukraine	Korea
6	US	Philippines	Singapore	Netherlands	US	Ireland	Japan
7	Korea	Indonesia	Australia	Finland	Denmark	Belarus	Romania
8	Iceland	Hungary	France	France	Norway	New Zealand	Italy
9	Germany	Czech Rep	Austria	Singapore	Australia	France	Moldova
10	Denmark	Finland	UK	Hong Kong	Luxembourg	UK	Armenia

Country	2012	2014
China	32	22
South Africa	33	49
Mexico	46	>50
Brazil	57	47
Egypt	61	>50

Care must be taken to not place too much emphasis on rankings and year-to-year movements. For example, although Switzerland's overall ranking declined from 2012 to 2014, it enjoyed substantial gains in "Manufacturing Capability," jumping from 15th in 2012 to 1st in 2014. Finland, Russia, and Korea topped the 2014 factor rankings for "R&D Intensity," "Tertiary Efficiency," and "Patent Activity," respectively; however, Bloomberg pointed out that although Russia has traditionally been "well educated" in science, math, and engineering, this has not necessarily turned the country into a global innovation powerhouse. Bloomberg also highlighted how countries such as Singapore and Korea had relied heavily on government-supported basic R&D to enhance their positions in the global innovation rankings.

MIT Technology Review

In 2013, the MIT Technology Review defined "innovation clusters" as "places with dense webs of interconnected technology companies, customers and suppliers" and identified the five largest regional technology clusters as Silicon Valley, Boston, Israel, Bangalore, and Beijing. The Review also noted the creation and development of Tech City in London, Saclay in Paris, and Skolkovo Innovation City in Russia as interesting government-supported efforts to fuel innovations in those countries.

Venture Source

Commentators often use venture capital activity as an indicator of a functioning entrepreneurial ecosystem. Data compiled by Dow Jones Venture Source in 2013 ranked the top venture capital funding "hotbeds" as follows (number in parentheses is amount of venture capital funding received by firms in country/region in 2012 express in billions of US dollars): San Francisco Bay Area, including Silicon Valley (11.2); New England, including Boston (3.6); Southern California (3.0); New York City Metro Area (2.4); UK (1.8); Beijing (1.5); Germany (1.0); Israel (1.0); France (0.9); Canada (0.8); Shanghai (0.6); Potomac Area, including Washington DC (0.6); Illinois (0.6), Bangalore (0.3); and Switzerland (0.3). It was notable that the top five hotbeds, the first four of which were in the US, brought in $22 billion, representing 53 percent of the global total for that year.

Global Innovation and Competitiveness Indexes

The top ten countries in The Global Innovation Index for 2012–2013 were as follows: Switzerland, Sweden, Singapore, Finland, United Kingdom, Netherlands, Denmark, Hong Kong, Ireland, and the United States. This list overlapped substantially with the following ten leaders in the World Economic Forum's Global Competitiveness Index for the same period: Switzerland, Finland, Sweden, Netherlands, Germany, United Kingdom, United States, Singapore, Hong Kong, and Japan.

Innovation is also factored into other international comparisons. For example, in 2014 the top countries with respect to "innovation" in the World Economic Forum's annual Global Competitiveness Index were, in order, Finland, Switzerland, Israel, Japan, US, Germany, Sweden, the Netherlands, Singapore, and Taiwan.[71] In contrast to the quantitative factors relied on in the Bloomberg measures, WEF rankings are compiled based on qualitative assessments grounded in responses to questionnaire circulated to 15,000 executives worldwide that seek views on issues such as innovation and labor market efficiency, sophistication of business sector, collaboration between academic and business sectors, company spending on research and development, intellectual property protection, effectiveness and transparency of public institutions, governance, infrastructure, functionality of goods markets, developed financial markets, and macroeconomic environment.[72]

---

[71] Id.

[72] Detailed profiles of all 144 economies included in the Global Competitiveness Index are available at the World Economic Forum's website.

World Startup Report

The Economist published a Special Report on Tech Startups in January 2014 that covered a number of topics relevant to the development of productive entrepreneurial ecosystems around the world including new strategies for testing a new business concept and launching new ventures, venture capital, "accelerators," business communities, founders, and hardware startups. The Report included a summary of data compiled by researchers working on a World Startup Report on the number of Internet firms in various countries around the world, including the number of firms valued at over $1 billion. The top ten countries on the list as of 2013, in order, included the following (number of firms valued at over $1 billion appears in parentheses): United States (87), China (26), Japan (11), UK (10), Korea (7), Israel (6), Russia (5), Australia (5), Brazil (4), and India (4).[73]

European Investment Hubs

A good of work has also been done on analyzing strengths and weaknesses of entrepreneurial ecosystems in various regions around the world. For example, the European Private Equity and Venture Capital Association published a report in 2013 on "The Case for Investing in European Venture Capital" that identified the following "Major European Investment Hubs": Barcelona, Belgium, Berlin, Denmark, Eindhoven, Helsinki, Ireland, London, Paris, Rhein-Main-Neckar, Silicon Fen, Stockholm, and Switzerland. According to the report, these cities, countries, and regions were attracting talent through collaboration among local entrepreneurs, funders, universities, and larger established technology companies.

---

[73] Business communities: All together now, *The Economist* (January 18, 2014), A Cambrian Moment: Special Report on Tech Startups 11. World Startup Report rankings in 2014 indicated that 30 countries have at least one Internet company who value has at one time exceeded $1 billion. Startup Nations. *The Economist* (July 12, 2014) 60.

Global Cities Report

Another interesting lens for viewing innovation around the world has been provided by the A.T. Kearney Global Cities report, which was launched in 2008 and most recently updated in 2015.[74] The 2015 edition of Global Cities included two parts—The Global Cities Index (GCI) and the Global Cities Outlook (GCO). The GCI assessed "global engagement" for 125 cities around the world and relied on 26 metrics in five dimensions: business activity, human capital, information exchange, cultural experience, and political engagement. The GCO, which appeared for the first time in 2015, evaluated the future potential of those same cities based on rates of change across four dimensions: personal well-being, economics, innovation, and governance.

The announcement of Global Cities 2015 reflected an emphasis on the GCO—the top five cities on that measure were, in order, San Francisco, London, Boston, New York, and Zurich—and highlighted the identification of 16 cities that were ranked in the top 25 of both the GCI and GCO, thus reflecting both strong current performance with respect to innovation and significant future potential. Members of this so-called "Global Elite" included New York, London, Los Angeles, Chicago, Toronto, San Francisco, Boston, Paris, Brussels, Berlin, Amsterdam, Tokyo, Singapore, Seoul, Sydney, and Melbourne. While most of the cities in the Global Elite were in developed countries, the A.T. Kearney consultants who authored the study noted that cities in China and India, especially Beijing, Ahmadabad, and New Delhi, were well positioned for the future. Other cities in the developing world showing rapid improvements included Kolkata and Mumbai in India, Ho Chi Minh City in Vietnam, Buenos Aires in Argentina, and Dubai. A commonly mentioned factor for advances among developing countries was improvements in human capital grounded in expansion of the number of inhabitants with tertiary degrees and better scores of their universities.

---

[74] For more information on the Global Cities 2015, go to https://atkearney.com/research-studies/global-cities-index

Index of the World's Most Dynamic Cities

JLL, a professional services company that specializes in real estate and investment management and which changed its name from Jones Lang LaSalle in 2014, issues an annual City Momentum Index (CMI) which lists "the world's most dynamic cities."[75] JLL explained that the CMI tracks the speed of change of economic conditions and commercial real estate markets in 134 established and emerging business hubs around the world, identifying those cities that have the most dynamic attributes over the short and long term. The CMI is based on 42 measures of dynamism, which are grouped into three main sub-indices:

- Socio-economic momentum, which is based on changes in city GDP, population, air passengers, corporate headquarters and foreign direct investment
- Commercial real estate momentum, which is based on changes in absorption, construction, rents, investment volumes and real estate transparency covering the office, retail and hotel sectors
- High-value incubators, which measure the ability of the underlying attributes of a city to maintain momentum over the longer term in terms of education, innovation, and environment (referred to by JLL as a city's "future-proofing capacity")

Cities that do well in the CMI are those that have the ability to embrace technological change, absorb rapid population growth, and strengthen global connectivity. The top ten cities in the 2017 CMI, in order, were: Bangalore, Ho Chi Minh City, Silicon Valley, Shanghai, Hyderabad, London, Austin, Hanoi, Boston, and Nairobi. High points of the survey results called out by JLL included the following:

---

[75] The discussion in this section is adapted from JLL's publication "What cities are changing fastest?: City Momentum Index 2017," available for download at http://jll.com/cities-research/City-Momentum

- India's Ascendancy: Not only was Bangalore ranked Number One, but also six Indian cities were included in the CMI Global Top 30 (more than any other country and replacing China as the leader).
- The Ubiquity of Technology: Technology and innovation were the strengths of many of the top cities in the CMI, including several medium-sized cities in the US that made the CMI Global Top 30: Austin, Boston, Seattle, San Francisco, and Raleigh-Durham.
- The Rise of Agile Emerging World Cities: JLL called out several cities in the CMI Global Top 30 as examples of cities that have been successfully transitioning to higher-value activities: Shanghai, Shenzhen, Dubai, Bangalore, and Hyderabad.
- Asian Hotspots and Dynamic City Clusters: Ho Chi Minh City and Hanoi, the two Vietnamese representatives in the top ten, were enjoying substantial interest from foreign investors, and clusters of dynamic cities were evolving in China (Shanghai, Hangzhou, and Nanjing) as inter-regional connectivity in that country improved.
- Future-Proofing of Northern European Cities: While European cities were largely absent from the Global Top 30, several of them (e.g., Stockholm, Berlin, Munich, and Amsterdam) demonstrated attributes to support longer-term momentum including specialized knowledge industries, strong educational institutions, and supportive living conditions.
- Challenges and Constraints: Poor environmental scores dampened the overall performance of some of the CMI Global Top 30 cities (e.g., Delhi and Beijing) and San Francisco and Hong Kong were each challenged and constrained by affordability and space constraints.

Emerging Markets

As for emerging markets, private equity investors have been noticeably active in Brazil, China, India, Korea, Mexico, Russia, South Africa, Turkey, and Vietnam, and researchers from the Wharton School reported an increasing interest in several other non-BRIC countries including Columbia, Chile, and Peru in Latin America, Kenya, and Nigeria in Africa, and Indonesia and Thailand in Asia.[76]

---

[76] Sammut, S. July 3, 2013. *Private Equity in Emerging Markets: Beyond the BRICs.* Beacon: Wharton Entrepreneurship Blog.

CHAPTER 3

Emerging Companies

Characteristics of Emerging Companies

It has become common to refer to technology-based entrepreneurial ventures as prospective "emerging companies" in large part because of their emphasis on, and potential for, high growth in both employment and revenues. While the term "emerging company" is now frequently used, particularly among professional firms and venture capital investors, there is still no widely accepted definition of the term and the characteristics of the firms that might fall within the scope of the definition. One place to begin in developing a working definition of "emerging company" is to recognize that it does not necessarily include every situation where one entrepreneur or a team of entrepreneurs attempts to overcome the trials and challenges that arise during the very earliest stages of conceiving and starting a new business (i.e., the "concept" stage). At a minimum, eligibility for emerging company status requires that the "next great idea" must have left the garage or the laptop in the attic and landed in its own discrete working space with human and financial resources obtained from outside the founder group. This is not necessarily an easy hurdle to overcome and it has been estimated that a large percentage of new firms are driven out of business before they reach their first anniversary.

Not all of the companies that survive the start-up phase would be considered "emerging." It is instructive to note that the terms "emerging company" and "emerging growth company" are often used interchangeably and this provides an important clue in distinguishing the types of firms that are of interest to us—in order to be an emerging company the resource base and organizational structure of the firm must be suitable for sustained growth and the founders, other senior managers and outside investors must have all targeted growth and expansion as a key goal in the overall strategy of the company. In addition, emerging companies are built on the assumption that the desired growth will come from some new and unforeseen development that totally changes the dynamics of the market in which they are competing—technological breakthroughs, dramatic shifts in the costs associated with satisfying existing consumer needs, identification of new consumer needs, and/or sociological or economic changes. It is the job of the managers of the emerging company to embrace and exploit these developments by identifying business opportunities and creating new products or services to take advantage of them.

Emerging companies are often distinguished from the broader set of entrepreneurial activities by focusing on the significant level of "innovation" associated with their business models. Researchers have attempted to identify those firms that have been most successful at innovation, and to describe and explain those business practices that tend to be associated with innovative companies. Presumably a listing of these practices can provide valuable clues for identifying emerging companies and the factors that are the best predictors of success. A survey of the research results relating to innovation reveals the following:

- Innovative companies have strong leaders that are able to clearly articulate a vision for the business, set targets and create and maintain open relationships with all stakeholders (i.e., customers, investors, suppliers, and employees).
- The most innovative companies have extensive knowledge of the marketplace, the needs of customers, and the strengths and weaknesses of their competitors.
- Innovative companies seek and retain extraordinarily qualified personnel, provide them with the proper amount of resources and general direction, and then allow them to make and pursue their own specific strategies for achieving the agreed goals.
- The organizational structure of an innovative company emphasizes integration of multiple disciplines and functions and teamwork, goal sharing, and full and effective communication of goals and objectives throughout the firm.
- Technology is used effectively throughout the company, including small changes in design, production processes, and customer services.

- The company strives and plans for continuous and constant innovation, as opposed to isolated new ideas, to improve and enhance products, services, and productivity.
- Innovative companies strive for strong brand recognition and rapid introduction of new products and services into the marketplace.
- Innovative companies have systems for collecting information about, and learning from, customers, competitors, and unrelated businesses around the world.

The research also identifies some of the most common specific strategies for innovation:

- Frequent implementation of new management techniques;
- Implementation of skill development and education programs for managers and employees;
- Regular introduction of new technologies, generally no less frequently than every three years;
- Constant and systematic benchmarking through regular comparison with the best companies in the industry and elsewhere;
- Significant investment in customer-focused product design and in quality-based manufacturing equipment and processes;
- Regular changes in the organization of work and administration, typically made in conjunction with the introduction of new products and/or technologies;
- Allocation of a significant share of turnover, generally at least 10 percent, to development and introduction of new products and processes; and
- Collaboration with universities and other research centers to identify technologies which can be converted into profitable products and processes.

It is now generally accepted that innovation is essential to continued productivity and economic growth; however, innovation in the form of uncovering a new technological breakthrough is not necessarily as important as how and when the technology is reduced to practice and diffused into the marketplace in the form of new or improved products and services. Successful emerging companies realize that the growth that they are pursuing must come through continuous creation, implementation and refinement of innovative business models and that the leaders in emerging markets will be those firms that can innovate—the companies that are successful in creating, acquiring, and/or combining technology and other knowledge into new products, services, or business processes faster and more efficiently than the competition. Many companies stall out and are unable to break through size and revenue plateaus because they are unable to keep their innovation engines churning. In order to be a successful emerging company a firm must constantly challenge their status quo and seek innovation with respect to its products and services and the processes that are used to add value for customers and other stakeholders.

Whether or not a particular company is "emerging" is sometimes assessed by reference to how the company stands with respect to certain key business and financial characteristics (see Table 3.1). These characteristics not only test the current and projected financial performance of the company—measured by revenues, sales, profit margin, cash flow, and so on, to determine whether the business has been, and will be, generating steadily increasing revenues at above-average rates, but also examine whether the company has the resources and strategies in place to grow rapidly. The sections that follow identify some of the key characteristics that companies must demonstrate in order to qualify as "emerging." The choice of topics was based on a wide array of sources including various publications that specialize in coverage of companies that have received support from venture capitalists. In addition, empirical information on the characteristics of emerging companies can be derived from a comprehensive study of the evolution of emerging companies by researchers from the University of Chicago Graduate School of Business that focused on how the characteristics of public companies that were launched with venture capital financing evolved from the date of their early business plan through their initial public offering (IPO) and on to mature public

Table 3.1 Characteristics of emerging companies

This is checklist of commonly noted characteristics of firms that would fit within the definition of an emerging company. The checklist can be a useful tool in preparing for presentations to potential investors, such as venture capitalists, that are focused on companies that have the potential for high returns on investment over a relatively finite holding period.

- Is the firm engaged in business activities that have combined innovation with extraordinary growth in turnover and employment?
- Is firm involved in the development and commercialization of new and innovative (i.e., emerging) technologies that promise to create entirely new markets or effect a substantial change in the competitive conditions that apply in specific existing markets?
- Does the firm have a distinctive competence in one or more areas that are essential to competitive success in its particular market [e.g., proprietary design technology (e.g., patents and trade secrets), manufacturing know-how, a unique brand, or extraordinary services]?
- Does the firm have core competencies based on human capital and other non-alienable assets such as knowledge and/or business processes?
- Does the firm engage in activities in a market that is expected to grow and expand rapidly in the future?
- Does the firm have a sensible and believable strategy for distributing its products and services within the target market?
- Is the firm involved in the development of relationships or contracts with recognized companies in the industry (i.e., "strategic alliances") that provide validation of the company's business model in the marketplace?
- Does the firm have innovative and unique products, processes, or services that can dominate a niche market segment?
- Does the firm have an internal growth strategy that focuses on continuous production of new or upgraded products during the early years of growth and evolution?
- Does the firm have a portfolio of proprietary intellectual property rights, such as patents, and physical assets?
- Are the actual or potential gross margins and/or cash flow generated by the company large enough to permit financing of growth over an extended period of time and produce a favorable return on invested capital?
- Does the firm have a full team of qualified, experienced, and credible senior managers?
- Does each member of the management team have experience in the target industrial and an entrepreneurial spirit?

status with the release of their third annual report following completion of their IPO.[1]

---

[1] See Kaplan, S., B. Sensoy, and P. Stromberg. 2005. *What are Firms? Evolution from Birth to Public Companies.* University of Chicago Graduate School of

Further information on how companies are classified as "emerging" can be obtained through a variety of publicly available resources. For example, the annual Inc. 500 list published by Inc. magazine identifies the 500 fastest-growing private companies in the United States according to specified criteria. While the magazine does provide profiles of many of the companies and additional information may be available through those firms in any other public resources it may be difficult to learn details of their specific strategies that can be used as guidance by entrepreneurs looking to build their own emerging companies. More information can be obtained with respect to "high growth" companies that have completed their IPO. One resource is Fortune's annual list of the 100 Fastest-Growing Companies, which is compiled based on various measures including market capitalization, stock price, duration of trading history, revenue and net income and compound annual growth in revenue and earnings per share over a three year period. Another source is the annual list of the 200 Best Small Companies published by *Forbes* magazine although not all of the listed companies would meet the quantitative criteria for "fastest-growing" status.

Business Activities

While innovation can, and does regularly, occur in any type of business, there are identifiable types of business activities that have combined innovation with extraordinary growth in turnover and employment, at least when compared to other entrepreneurial firms. These businesses typically have a technology-based focus in their products, services, and processes. In fact, among the industrial classifications characterized as emerging companies are the following: manufacturers of pharmaceuticals, medical and chemical products; manufacturers of computers and other data

---

Business. Other results from the study provided interesting contributions to identifying the stages of development through which successful emerging companies passed as they completed their IPO and settled into mature public company status. For discussion, see "Managing Growth and Change: A Library of Resources for Sustainable Entrepreneurs" prepared and distributed by the Sustainable Entrepreneurship Project (www.seproject.org).

processing equipment; manufacturers of electrical machinery and apparatus; manufacturers of communications equipment, including radio and television; manufacturers of medical, precision, and optical instruments; and developers and distributors of software and related computer services.

Technology

The term "emerging company" is most often associated with firms involved in the development and commercialization of new and innovative (i.e., emerging) technologies that promise to create entirely new markets or effect a substantial change in the competitive conditions that apply in specific existing markets. In many instances there is significant uncertainty, often outright skepticism, regarding the scientific and engineering basis for the new technology and it may unclear what benefits and functions will actually be derived from the technology if the initial development work can even be completed. Another complicating factor is that companies will be laboring in areas where there is no consensus on accepted standards.

Products and Services

Consistent with the focus on emerging technologies, emerging companies are expected to have innovative distinctive products, services or processes that can dominate, and often pioneer, a niche market segment. Ideally the company can begin commercialization of its products immediately following completion of development without delays caused by regulatory hurdles; however, biotechnology and life sciences companies certainly fall within the definition of emerging companies even though they generally must wait several years before their products are approved for release to the public. It is also a positive sign if customers must make recurring purchases of the company's products and services.

Market

While the initial vision of the benefits and functions of, and corresponding market for products based on, the technologies being developed by an emerging company may be cloudy, eventually the firm must be able to demonstrate the potential to achieve annual revenues of at least $50 million on a profitable basis within three years after launch and ultimately attain a market valuation in excess of $1 billion within five years after launch. While the current size of the market is relevant the more important consideration is whether the market is expected to grow and expand rapidly in the future and, in fact, many require that the company be competing in an industry that itself is considered to be "emerging." A related issue is whether the company has a sensible and believable strategy for distributing its products and services within the target market.

Origin of Business Idea

In the University of Chicago study group the two most common sources for the origin of the business idea underlying the new company were ideas developed by the founders from experience with previous employers and academic research. A small group of companies traced their beginnings to a spin-off of, or joint venture with, an existing company. Certain industries, such as biotechnology, were more likely to be grounded in academic research than ideas from previous employment. Other researchers have analyzed the source of business ideas for venture-capital financed companies and other fast growing small businesses such as firms found on the annual list of the 500 fastest-growing companies published by Inc. magazine (i.e., the so-called "Inc. 500"). In one instance the researcher found that while companies backed by venture capitalists were more likely to have innovative ideas and a verifiable record of achievement, a high percentage of Inc. 500 companies in a particular year (1989) were launched based on ideas that the founders had identified during the course of their prior employment and elected to replicate or modify to form the basis of their new company. The researcher opined that since the Inc. 500 companies were generally formed and launched with relatively small amounts of advance planning they were more likely than venture capital-financed firm to go through adjustments in their business models as they worked to grow the company and find their niche in the marketplace.[2]

---

[2] Bhide, A. 2000. *The Origin and the Evolution of New Businesses,* 111. New York, NY: Oxford University Press.

Earnings and Dividends

Actual or potential gross margins and/or cash flow should be large enough to permit financing of growth over an extended period of time, and produce a favorable return on invested capital. An emerging company is expected to seek and obtain a faster rate of earning growth than the "average" company. For example, if and when the shares of the company are traded in the public markets the target growth rate for earnings should be significantly higher than the Standard & Poor's 500 Stock Index and investors will typically expect earnings growth of at least 15 percent, but usually 20 percent or higher, over the next three to five years. Earnings growth, and the attendant rise in share prices, is important to investors since the expectation is that profits will be reinvested in the business to sustain the extraordinary level of earnings growth and thus will not be available to fund more than nominal or occasional cash dividend distributions. When preparing financial projections management should demonstrate an understanding and mastery of the key assumptions upon which the projections are based and must also demonstrate that consideration use been given to potential adverse developments that might trigger a need to quickly shift the strategic business plan.

Founders' Goals and Characteristics

While some firms appear to stumble into the explosive growth associated with being an "emerging company" the general rule is that the pursuit of growth is a path that is explicitly chosen during the early stages of the firm's existence. One group of researchers has argued that growth, rather than being an inevitable phase as depicted in many of models of firm evolution, is actually a result of a conscious decision made by the owner/founder/CEO of the firm which is based, in part, on his or her assessment of whether or not he or she will actually be able to manage the anticipated or desired growth of the business.[3] The same researchers found

---

[3] Sexton, D., and N. Bowman-Upton. 1986. "Validation of a Personality Index: Comparative Psychological Characteristics Analysis of Female Entrepreneurs, Managers, Entrepreneurship Students and Business Students." In *Frontiers of Entrepreneurship Research*, eds. R. Ronstadt et al. Wellesley, MA: Babson College.

evidence that growth-oriented entrepreneurs scored higher on indicators of energy level, risk-taking, social adroitness, autonomy, and change than their non-growth oriented counterparts and scored lower on indicators of conformity, interpersonal affect, harm avoidance, and succorance. It is not enough, however, to have the psychological traits normally associated with an orientation for growth, since the owner/founder/CEO is not likely to be successful unless he or she is also able to acquire and manage the various resources necessary for the firm to meet its growth targets and objectives, including capital, labor, and technology.

Business Strategy

Several researchers have identified similar categories of business strategies that can be used to differentiate new companies. A common methodology uses the following five classifications for business strategies—innovators, enhancers, marketers, technology/marketing hybrids, and cost.[4] Innovators include firms that compete on the basis of creating and selling novel products for new and undeveloped markets. Enhancers are firms that compete by creating and selling improvements and enhancements to existing products that are already established in developed markets. Marketers compete based on building and maintaining core competencies in marketing, sales, and distribution. Technology/marketing hybrids use strategies that combine elements of technology (i.e., innovators and enhancers) and marketers. Cost-focused firms seek competitive differentiation by following strategies of reducing the costs of producing and marketing their products. The sample used by Baron et al. in a study published in 1999 rendered a distribution among 149 firms as follows: innovators (50 percent), enhancers (19 percent), marketers (13 percent), technology/marketing hybrids (12 percent), and cost (7 percent).[5] The smaller sample group of 49 companies used by the researchers in the University of Chicago study showed a similar breakdown: innovators (49

[4] Baron, J., M. Hannan, and M. Burton. 1999. "Building the Iron Cage: Determinants of Managerial Intensity in the Early Years of Organizations." *American Sociological Review* 64, pp. 527–47.

[5] Id.

percent), enhancers (22 percent), marketers (10 percent), technology/
marketing hybrids (12 percent), and cost (6 percent).

Management

Probably the most important success factor for any business is the presence of qualified, experienced, and credible management and this is especially true in the case of emerging companies since they must face and
overcome turbulent and challenging conditions as they move quickly
through several growth stages. Ideally, the founder(s) and other senior
managers should be experienced in the target industry and each of them
must demonstrate a strong entrepreneurial spirit and dedicated focus on
the business. In any event, the company must have a management team
in place rather than just one person acting as the CEO. The management
team must also be able to articulate a clear and aggressive strategic plan
for future growth and competitive entry into key market segments. Since
early investors seek a high profile exit strategy (i.e., an IPO or acquisition
by a public company) the members of the management team must have
a good reputation and experience dealing with the challenges of positioning the firm for a major liquidity event when the opportunity arises.

Point of Differentiation

The point of differentiation refers to the factors that companies identify as
allowing them to differentiate themselves from their competitors—their
unique strategic advantage or "distinctive competence." Not surprisingly,
the most important factor mentioned by the emerging companies in the
University of Chicago study group at all points along their path of evolution was a unique product and/or technology. This is similar to other
reports that emphasized that venture capitalists, the primary source of
funding for the companies in the University of Chicago study group,
predominantly look for and invest in new businesses based on proprietary
products and services.[6] As time goes on, the companies also began to

---

[6] See, for example, Bhide, A. 2000. *The Origin and the Evolution of New Businesses*. New York, NY: Oxford University Press. Among venture capitalists there
is a discernable split of opinion as to whether the key determinant of success

place increasingly higher importance on customer service as a strategy for differentiation. Less important factors, although statistically significant at all stages of growth, included breadth of product line, strategic alliances/ partnerships, and reputation. Other researchers have cited manufacturing "know-how" supported by proprietary processes as an important and valuable core competency.

Even though a large percentage of the emerging companies in the study group believed that they had a unique product and/or technology, 84 percent of those companies acknowledged that they expected to face competition in their target markets at the point of the earliest business plan and all of the companies in the study group, including those that opted for another point of differentiation noted that competition was going to be a factor in determining their success by the time that they reached the IPO stage. For a majority of the emerging companies in the study group the type of competition remained stable over time; however, a large minority (40 percent) noted that competition broadened as time went by and markets developed.

The feedback with respect to the importance of expertise of senior management and other employees, also mentioned in the context of asset stability as emerging companies evolve and mature,[7] is interesting enough to warrant separate consideration. As of the date of the early business plan, 45 percent of the companies in the University of Chicago study group expressly referred to expertise as being an important differentiating factor. While this was far less than the unanimous designation of unique

---

for emerging companies is the targeted product and market or the strength and experience of the management team. While the preferred situation is to invest in a company that has promise on each of these dimensions, it appears that different venture capital firms usually assign more weight to one factor than the other. See, for example, Kaplan, S., and P. Stromberg. 2004. "Characteristics, Contracts, and Actions: Evidence from Venture Capitalist Analyses." *Journal of Finance* 59, no. 5, pp. 2177–210; and Quindlen, R. 2000. *Confessions of a Venture Capitalist.* New York, NY: Warner Books.

[7] For detailed discussion of asset stability as emerging companies evolve and mature, see "Managing Growth and Change: A Library of Resources for Sustainable Entrepreneurs" prepared and distributed by the Sustainable Entrepreneurship Project (www.seproject.org).

products and/or technology as a differentiating factor, it was more than any other factor at that stage; however, it is interesting to note that less than half of the companies in the study failed to assign importance to expertise as a means of differentiation. The University of Chicago researchers found a notable and marked decrease in the percentage of companies that cited expertise to be important at the time of the IPO (14 percent) and at the time of the third annual report following the IPO (13 percent) and cited this as evidence that non-human capital factors become more important than human capital as emerging companies mature.

Organizational Design and Structure

The unique goals and objectives of emerging companies, particularly their emphasis on technology and innovation as core competencies and points of differentiation, must be supported by appropriate practices with respect to organizational design and structure.[8] Jelinek and Schoonhoven found that companies that were the most successful in pursuing a strategy of innovation tended to consciously work to encourage the free flow of new and innovative ideas from many sources and involve employees from all levels of the organization in the selection of ideas to pursue. While emerging companies do create formal organizational structures that define reporting channels and responsibility for decisions in various areas, they differ from traditional bureaucratic organizations in that structure is seen as a flexible tool that can, and should, be easily changed as circumstances warrant.[9]

Warrick argued that the appropriate organizational design for the dynamic environment in which technology-based firms (i.e., emerging companies) must operate should achieve the following goals: alignment of the structure, particularly the performance review and reward systems,

---

[8] For detailed discussion of various topics relating to organizational design and structure, see "Organizational Design: A Library of Resources for Sustainable Entrepreneurs" prepared and distributed by the Sustainable Entrepreneurship Project (www.seproject.org).

[9] Jelinek, M., and C. Schoonhoven. 1990. *The Innovation Marathon*. Oxford: Basil Blackwell.

to be consistent with the mission, philosophy and goals of the firm; assuring that the right people are in the right place with clear responsibilities; assuring that skilled leaders and managers are placed in key positions; and developing a lean, flexible, non-bureaucratic, functional, and results-oriented structure that encourages self-management, high productivity, and innovation.[10]

Warrick also noted other characteristics of the typical high technology firm that need to be taken into account in the organizational design process. For example, since these companies generally have a high proportion of technical employees, most of whom prefer to be left alone to pursue their job and give little or no priority to planned change throughout the firm, it is important for senior management to champion change programs and educate all employees about the importance of the program and the need for all levels of the organization to embrace each of the initiatives associated with the program. Small technology-based growth firms also suffer from a lack of experienced management. Accordingly, in order for the firm to be able to survive in its dynamic environment, conscious effort needs to be made to train and develop managers throughout the organization. In particular, emphasis should be placed on providing managers with the skills and techniques to effectively manage small teams and specific projects. Finally, while change is a concept that begins at the top of the organization, change programs must be designed and promoted in a way that addresses and satisfies the needs of individual employees for ownership and personal growth.

Additional input regarding the appropriate focus on organizational design and structure for emerging companies came from Kolodny, who suggested the following list of the most common organizational forms for new technology-based firms: project management systems; matrix organizations; organismic; network organizations; product focused; and functional forms with teams.[11]

---

[10] Warrick, D. 1990. "How to Develop a High Tech Firm into a High Performance Organization." *Which appears in Organizational Issues in High Technology Management*, eds. L.R. Gomez-Mejia and M.W. Lawless, 151–63. Greenwich, CT: JAI Press Inc.

[11] Kolodny, H. 1990. "Characteristics of Organizational Designs in New/High Technology Firms." Which appeared In *Organizational Issues in High Technology*

Extensive literature has developed on both project management systems and matrix organizations.[12] One example of an organismic organizational structure relies on the creation of several marketing-based groups that have primary responsibility for new product development and marketing activities in a particular product or market sector. Each group is also supported by engineering and manufacturing resources; however, the firm also creates and maintains separate groups specifically dedicated to developing and understanding new technology and manufacturing processes. Once a product has been completed and enters the manufacturing stage, production issues are handled almost entirely at the factory or plant level and each product unit is kept to a reasonable size in order to facilitate effective control. The headquarters office assumes primary responsibility for the finance, human resource, and legal functions and also sets the strategic direction for the entire business.[13]

The use of "networking" refers to the common practice among small high technology firms of collaborating with other companies to bid on large contracts. By so doing, the firm is able to address gaps in its own resource base that might otherwise prevent it from pursuing those contracts. Over time, the firm develops trusted and reliable relationships with several partners and taps into their resources rather than investing in the internal development of comparable assets and skills. There are several different ways of classifying and explaining product-focused organizational forms, including semi-autonomous work groups, group technology cells, parallelization and product shops. Key characteristics of a

---

Management, eds. L. Gomez-Mejia and M. Lawless, 165–76. Greenwich, CT: JAI Press Inc.

[12] See, for example, Cleland, D., and W. King. 1982. *Product Management Handbook*. New York, NY: Van Nostrand Reinhold; and Cleland, D., and W. King. 1985. *Matrix Management Handbook*. New York, NY: Van Nostrand Reinhold. See also "Organizational Design: A Library of Resources for Sustainable Entrepreneurs" prepared and distributed by the Sustainable Entrepreneurship Project (www.seproject.org).

[13] Kolodny, H. 1990. "Characteristics of Organizational Designs in New/High Technology Firms." Which appeared in *Organizational Issues in High Technology Management*, eds. L. Gomez-Mejia and M. Lawless, 165–176, 168. Greenwich, CT: JAI Press Inc.

product-focused organization include the use of new process manufacturing technology, computer integrated manufacturing, and changes in materials and inventory management practices.[14]

Strategic Alliances

Emerging companies must have, or be in the process of developing, relationships or contracts with recognized companies in the industry in order to demonstrate the credibility of the company's business model in the marketplace. Strategic alliances can provide access to technology and other needed resources and allow the company to scale up its manufacturing and sales activities quickly without having to make substantial capital investments. In fact, within the University of Chicago study group there was an increase in the use of strategic alliances from the time of the earliest business plan to the IPO; however, usage appeared to flatten out over the three years following completion of the IPO. Nonetheless, 69 percent of the companies remained involved in one or more strategic alliances at the time of the third annual report following the IPO and reliance on alliances was even higher in some industries such as biotechnology.[15]

Location

Studies show that there is a high concentration of successful, and potential, emerging companies in a small number of geographic areas that appear to have the requisite infrastructure to spawn and nurture these types of businesses. Silicon Valley in California is probably the best example of an area where there seems to be a magical nexus of talent, money, innovation and lifestyle factors and other areas where an extraordinarily high level of innovative activity has occurred include Austin (Silicon Hills), Boston (Route 128), New York (Silicon Alley), Portland (Silicon Forest), and San

---

[14] Id. at p. 170.
[15] For further discussion of strategic alliances and other partnerships, see "Managing Growth and Change: A Library of Resources for Sustainable Entrepreneurs" prepared and distributed by the Sustainable Entrepreneurship Project (www.seproject.org).

Diego (Silicon Coast). The conditions for the creation of a Silicon Valley have been well documented and include access to universities, substantial involvement in government-funded research and development activities, venture capital, and an attractive environment for talented employees.

Emerging Companies in Foreign Countries

While the term "emerging companies" originated as a descriptor for certain types of firms launched and located in the US, it is clear that new technologies, products, and business models are continuously flowing from all parts of the world and that emerging companies can now be found almost anywhere including countries where the overall economy is itself referred to as "emerging." Entrepreneurs in those countries must certainly strive to meet certain essential universal requirements for emerging company status—technology, products, markets, and distinctive competencies—and must also demonstrate that their ventures can compete with established competitors from mature, industrialized areas. In particular, these firms must concentrate on investing in new equipment and technology, complying with internationally-accepted quality standards, implementing effective financial management and investment strategies, and adhering to accounting standards and practices that are understood and accepted in the US and other industrialized countries. It also important for the leaders of innovative firms in emerging markets to proactively pressure local government officials to create a political and business environment that foreign investors perceive as stable and transparent.

The Global Entrepreneurship Monitor (GEM) is a partnership between the London Business School and Babson College that administers a comprehensive research program to produce annual assessments of national levels of entrepreneurial activity.[16] An integral part of these assessments is the collection and analysis of data from around the world on "high-expectation entrepreneurs," which should be understood to

---

[16] For further information on the Global Entrepreneurship Monitor, see "Research on Entrepreneurship" in "Entrepreneurship: A Library of Resources for Sustainable Entrepreneurs" prepared and distributed by the Sustainable Entrepreneurship Project (www.seproject.org).

include entrepreneurs that either expect to employ at least 20 employees within five years of starting a new firm, and on "high-growth entrepreneurs," which are entrepreneurs that have been in business over 42 months and who currently employ 20 or more employees. In 2007, for example, the GEM researchers reported that in addition to the US, the following countries ranked in a global "Top 10" with respect to their rates of high-expectation and high-growth entrepreneurs in their adult populations: China, New Zealand, Iceland, Canada, Argentina, Australia, Singapore, Israel, and Ireland.

An interesting subject for comparison with the US is the United Kingdom, which has been at the forefront of developing a national portfolio of technology-based companies and ranked 11th in the 2007 GEM report referred to above.[17] The British Venture Capital Association (BVCA) has reported that the venture capital industry in the UK is the largest and most developed in Europe and second to the US in world importance. Surveys available from the BVCA have indicated that venture-backed companies in the UK have been able to dramatically exceed the national growth rate for all businesses with respect to increased staffing levels, sales, export, and investment, and it has been estimated that these companies have employed as must as 15 percent of the private sector workforce in the United Kingdom. In recent years, a significant portion of the IPO activities on the Official List of the London Stock Exchange have been private equity based companies. Specific geographic areas, particularly London and the South East, have benefited substantially from investment by professional venture capitalists and the successes experienced in and around Cambridge and Oxford have been well documented. However, while these reports are impressive, information collected and reported during the late 2000s indicated that the number of technology-related companies in the US that received venture capital financing was significantly greater than the comparable number in the UK and that UK investment in high technology companies was still substantially less than the amount invested in such companies in the US.

---

[17] Parts of the discussion of emerging companies in the UK in this section are adapted from Gutterman, A. 2003. *Advising New Businesses: A Practical Guide.* London: Sweet & Maxwell Group Ltd.

A comparison of the strategies and growth patterns of emerging companies in the US and the UK as of the late 2000s revealed several interesting differences. For example, while research and development expenditures in both countries were roughly comparable, UK technology-based companies continued to favor defense-related initiatives while US companies were more likely to search for commercial applications. At the time of their IPO, emerging companies in the US tended to have a much higher level of revenues than their counterparts in the UK. This may be explained by the fact that US firms could tap into larger domestic markets, thereby generating higher levels of revenue, while emerging companies in the UK need to explore and enter new foreign markets much earlier in the development cycle. The level of venture capital ownership at the time of the IPO was higher in the US than in the UK, a finding that could be explained, in part, by the historical reluctance of venture capitalists in the UK to invest in what are perceived to be "higher risk" companies. In addition, at the time of the IPO the percentage of equity owned by employees in the US was much higher than in the UK, which reflected the practice of companies in the US to grant options almost immediately following beginning of employment while UK companies moved more slowly in diluting the ownership share of the founding group by granting an equity interest to employees.

The apparent dynamism of the venture capital community in the UK was interesting given the overall profile of entrepreneurial aspirations in that country. In general, surveys taken in recent years by the GEM indicated that a relatively small percentage of the entrepreneurs in the UK anticipated that they would create 20 or more jobs as their business develops. In 2001, for example, this percentage was just 14 percent and, in addition, only about 3 percent of the existing start-up businesses at that time expected growth to more than 50 employees, putting it at the bottom of the top third and well behind countries such as the Netherlands (7 percent), Norway (7 percent), and the US (5 percent). As to new firms launched in 2000 and 2001, 11 percent of those in the UK projected high growth to over 50 employees; however, the equivalent rate in the US was 39 percent and in Australia it was 42 percent. While the UK was on the same level as France and Germany in each of these measures, it lagged well behind Canada, Ireland, Russia, and Sweden, as well as the other countries referred to above.

As is the case in the US, the inertia for creation of emerging companies in other countries tends to be most prominent in specific geographic areas where technology-driven firms appear to cluster. It has been persuasively argued that geography "matters" when searching for innovative activity. For example, it has been observed that "[i]ndustrial agglomerations located in one place, rather than some other, create environments in which production experience can be accumulated, exchanged, and preserved in the local workforce and entrepreneurial community."[18] In another study of the impact of geography on innovation in the US, the researcher argued that innovation arises from the dynamic interaction of multiple technological infrastructures in a particular location as opposed to the activities of any single firm.[19]

Encouragement and support of technology-driven firms can be, and has become, an important strategy for economic development in smaller countries that need to pursue different strategies in order to achieve sustainable growth due to their size and relative disadvantages in relation to the larger nations. Smaller countries cannot build a domestic economy that is large enough to support a highly differentiated industrial base. This is particularly true with respect to industries that require growth to a level in which economies of scale can be achieved in order for participants to be competitive on a global scale (e.g., steel and automobiles). Import protection policies are of little value in these circumstances since the domestic market will never be large enough to fully support local firms and such firms will inevitably need to look outward for global trading opportunities in order to integrate their domestic activities with larger markets in order to achieve continuous growth.

Small countries, as well as regional economies in larger nations, are confronted with special problems and disadvantages in forging an effective science and technology policy. The major issue, of course, is the

---

[18] David, P.A., and D. Foray. 1995. "Accessing and Expanding the Science and Technology Base." *STI Review* 16. OECD Periodical.

[19] Feldman, M.P. 1994. *The Geography of Innovation*. Dordrecht: Kluwer Academic.

relative lack of capital and other resources that may be available to invest in research and development. In addition, smaller countries obviously lack a large domestic market that can be exploited to obtain economies of scale and increase the chances of obtaining profitability for internal research and development project. As a result, they must selectively choose those opportunities where they can make the most efficient use of their resources. Generally, this requires the following:

- Identification of specialized market and technology niches in which the country or region can compete effectively against larger countries;
- Identification of research and development opportunities where the initial barriers to entry are low and economies of scale are less important;
- Adoption of policies that encourage cooperation with, and inbound investment by, larger foreign firms that are willing to provide technology and facilitate development of local business networks that include smaller indigenous firms; and
- Development and implementation of domestic policies that encourage rapid commercial deployment of the results of research and development activities and diffusion of new technologies throughout the local industrial base.

Even these solutions, when implemented, come with some degree of risk. For example, the need to maintain an "open economy," while important for attracting foreign investment and technology, means that it is more difficult for indigenous firms to preserve any technological advantage they may have developed in niche areas.

Small countries are particularly dependent on inbound transfers as a means for acquiring world-class technologies necessary to raise living standards and develop and produce products and services that will be successful in global markets since these countries lack the institutions generally found in the US and other larger countries that are required to develop the necessary technologies. In order for those countries to be successful in creating the environment necessary for emerging companies to flourish the following conditions must be meant to attract profitable foreign direct investment:

- Low corporate tax rate and/or special tax incentives for foreign investment into targeted industry sectors;
- Liberal regulatory policies with respect to inbound foreign investment, including opportunities for foreign investors to retain 100 percent ownership of domestic operations;
- Low tariff duties on the importation of capital goods and intermediate products necessary for production activities in the export sector;
- Exchange rate policies that allow the country to maintain competitive wage levels in relation to other potential foreign production centers;
- Adequate infrastructure (i.e., power, ports, and warehousing) and efficient administrative service (i.e., customs and taxation) to ensure that domestically manufactured products can be efficiently disseminated into world markets;
- Stable political environment with low risk of expropriation of volatile regulation policies and practices;
- Low rates of government expenditure as a percentage of national GDP, thereby facilitating low taxation rates and higher private sector savings and investment;
- Competitive labor markets, including low payroll taxes, low or no minimum wage requirements, and regulatory flexibility with respect to recruiting and dismissing employees as required by business conditions; and
- Favorable geographic position, thereby reducing the costs of inbound shipments for suppliers and outbound transport for finished products into target export markets.

The importance of any of these factors will be influenced by the particular products and the markets therefore. For example, many countries that have thrived on the manufacture of electronics products that are eventually re-sold into highly developed countries such as the US must rely almost exclusively on imported components that represent a very high percentage of the final export value of the products. If the country was to impose even a small tariff on imports of such components, or failed to provide a cost-effective transportation infrastructure, foreign investors would abandon the country quickly to find a more cost-effective alternative.

Another interesting phenomenon that has occurred in recent years as a truly interdependent global economy has emerged has been the accelerated focus in many developing countries on achieving growth and progress in their industrial sectors. For example, many countries in Eastern Europe, eager for integration into the broader European Union, unleashed ambitious modernization plans; however, success has not been easy or quick due to challenges raised by the following problems in those countries: backward industrial structure and lack of a critical mass of local businesses that are dependent on scientific and technological developments; outdated technology and low levels of innovation; poor labor productivity; significant dependence on cheap materials from neighboring countries; lack of professional and managerial competence; poor cooperation among various economic sectors and lack of competitiveness in key business infrastructure areas such as energy and distribution; and poor infrastructure for business services and poorly developed financial services sector. In order to succeed, such countries must be willing and able to make the transition from physical product to business and information services and develop global, as opposed to strictly domestic or regional, markets for the products and services. In addition, developing countries must look to shift their focus from industrial areas to the creation of competitive clusters.

Managing Emerging Companies

Emerging companies, particularly when they are at their earlier stages, have a number of strengths that distinguish them from larger companies. Among other things, the founders and other managers of small emerging companies often demonstrate exceptional determination to be successful, creating an enthusiasm that permeates the entire organization. In general, the innovation process is much more rapid in these firms and they are generally able to respond more quickly to customer needs. In many cases, initial success is achieved by identifying and servicing niche markets that have been ignored by larger companies. Smaller firms can also thrive by taking on jobs that are considered to be too small for bigger businesses.

On the other hand, some of the very characteristics that create opportunities for small emerging companies can endanger their survival. For example, the limited resources and day-to-day pressures of launching a new business often leads to a short-term focus and neglect of the investment in human resources necessary for long-term success and stability. Small firms may also become too reliant on a small group of customers. Cash flow is another common problem for firms in the early stages, since they are particularly vulnerable to order stoppages and slow payment by a single customer and generally experience difficulties in finding capital required for expansion on reasonable terms. Finally, while governments are attempting to reduce the regulatory burdens confronting small businesses, the time and costs of compliance are still disproportionately high for companies of this size.

Small businesses engaged in technology-related innovation face additional challenges above and beyond the hurdles confronting other small firms. For example, they must find a way to collect development capital to complete the work necessary to move into the production and diffusion phase. This is often problematic in that such firms must survive for substantial periods with revenues from commercial activities. Also, success in this type of venture requires an unusual mix of technical and managerial abilities that differ from the generic group of small businesses. In particular, the ability to effectively transfer technology developed in a science-based environment into new commercial applications is essential to the growth of innovative technology firms. Finally, small technology-based firms tend to be more reliant on networking relationships with other firms and organizations (e.g., universities) having complimentary resources.

In light of these challenges, it is not surprising that the early years of existence are tremendously volatile for new firms. In fact, various studies have indicated that 30 percent of the new firms launched in the United Kingdom were out of business by the third year following formation and the number increased to 50 percent by the fifth year. Of those firms that are able to survive only a small number grew beyond 20 employees. In order to achieve the desired growth rate, or to simply just survive, new businesses must be able to develop appropriate management skills, attract sufficient capital, and make the right strategic decisions with respect to creation, acquisition, and marketing of their products and services.

Critical Success Factors

The risks associated with emerging companies have led to keen interest in attempting to identify the critical success factors that are likely to be relevant in predicting how a particular firm will fare in the marketplace. The term critical success factors in the context of a business organization can be understood as referring to the primary process performance measures that most closely define and track how the organization must perform in order to be considered successful. In order to be effective and meaningful the critical success factors for a company must be directly related to the business and strategic objectives and goals of the company as set out in a formal business plan and must also be defined in a way that they can be easily monitored by senior management to quickly determine whether the company is "on track." One common analogy used with respect to setting and reviewing performance against key indicators is the instruments commonly found on the dashboard of an automobile or an airplane.

It is admittedly difficult to measure performance, and establish critical success factors, in the early days of a new venture that has been launched based on an emerging technology that will hopefully create markets that do not currently exist. At that point the various entrepreneurs (i.e., the founders and other senior managers) lack the traditional points of reference typically used to design critical success factors—there are no products on the market, the market itself is still be evaluated and defined, competition has yet to emerge, standards are lacking, and decisions have yet to be made regarding the involvement of regulators and the boundaries of property rights that may be associated with new technologies. What often occurs is that a list of milestones or benchmarks is created to serve as a roadmap of the path of events that need to be completed in order to achieve "success": close the first round of venture capital funding, complete development and testing of the initial product, establish of one or more key strategic alliances, successfully launch the initial product, rollout additional products, and complete a successful IPO. A target date is assigned to each milestone and a detailed list of the activities that need to be undertaken to reach each milestone is also created.

Certainly each of the events listed above is important; however, they are more correctly viewed as the desirable consequences of having identifying and managing critical success factors rather than being success factors in and of themselves. For example, it is more accurate to identify what they company should be doing in order to obtain financial resources from venture capitalists or complete and launch its first product efficiently and on a timely basis. These "factors for success," which should be the subject of measurement as indicators of performance, might include establishment of an organizational structure and project management capability to support operational activities or creation of a high-quality new product development process. It should also be noted that achieving a certain benchmark may itself improve performance with respect to a critical success factor. A good illustration is the expected improvements in process development that a smaller company can expect from absorbing knowledge from larger and more experience partners during the course of a strategic alliance relationship.

Not surprisingly, the search to identify critical success factors for fledgling technology-based companies has spread far and wide and there have been numerous studies on the subject. In general, research in the area of critical success factors for emerging companies has focused on the identification and studies of two main groups of factors: "internal" factors, which focus on the characteristics of the particular company and its founders and senior managers which can usually be affected by the company itself; and "contextual" (or external) factors, which focus on the organizational environment in which the company is operating and generally exist independent of the activities of the company although management generally has some discretion in defining key elements of the organizational environment in which the company will be operating. Each main group can be further broken down into specific categories for closer analysis. For example, internal factors might be classified by reference to human resources, product development strategies, organization structure and culture, and stakeholder relationships. In turn, contextual factors include the creation and operation of regional clusters of firms working on related issues, the breadth and condition of the infrastructure supporting the activities of the company (e.g., transportation, telecommunications, availability of affordable housing, and so on), and governmental policies relating to the technologies and markets of interest to the company. There will obviously be some overlap between internal and contextual factors such as whether the local housing market is attractive enough to support the company's efforts to recruit the personnel deemed critically necessary for success.

Internal Factors

The success or failure of a new business venture will ultimately depend, to some extent, on the skills, energy, and judgment of the founders and the other members of the senior management team. These factors, including the personal characteristics and experience of the members of the founder-manager team and the specific strategies that they select to cope with their company's business environment, are typically classified as "internal," since they are integral part of the firm itself and the way it is managed. Outside investors who place the greatest emphasis on internal factors are said to fall into the camp of basing their bets on the "jockey" (i.e., the management team) rather than on the "horse" (i.e., the business model). For example, Arthur Rock, a revered investor who was one of the first to see the promise in Apple Computers, has often been cited for this belief that the quality, integrity, and commitment of the members of the management team is the most important factor in an investment decision. Others have taken a similar view by favorably quoting the following saying: "You can have a good idea and poor management and lose every time. You can have a poor idea and good management and win every time."[20] However, other studies have shown that once a firm emerges from the very earliest stages of development the company's ultimate success is determined by non-human factors such as intellectual property rights, customer relationships, and physical assets and firms with the right product in the right market will thrive even if there is substantial change within the management team.

---

[20] Gladstone, D. 2002. *Venture Capital Handbook*, 91–92. Financial Times Prentice Hall.

Not surprisingly, various studies have focused on certain personal characteristics of the founders and other managers of a company in an effort to predict whether the company would be able to achieve rapid growth. For example, Barkham et al. argued that there is a significant positive correlation between faster growth and characteristics such as the relative youth of the ownership group; shared ownership and cooperation, meaning that more than one person had an equity stake in the business and that there was a willingness to work together as a group; serial entrepreneurship among the founder-manager group, meaning that members of the group have been involved in more than one business activity; and membership in professional organizations, which generally meant that the founders and managers had achieved recognized levels of technical competence and certification (e.g., engineering).[21] Storey evaluated empirical studies of founder-manager teams conducted by a number of other researchers and concluded that the most commonly-cited predictors of rapid growth for companies led by those teams included relatively high levels of education and extensive management experience from previous positions. Storey also noted that the companies that were most likely to be successful in achieving high growth were led by a team or group of entrepreneurs, rather than just one individual, and that the leadership team was usually middle-aged, a finding that was somewhat at variance with Barkham et al. but consistent with advanced education and management experience.[22]

In contrast, advocates of the strategic management theory posit that the most important internal factors are not the personal characteristics of the founders and other members of the management team but the actual choices made by those persons with respect to charting the course for the business in light of the relevant environmental conditions. This approach is consistent with the belief that entrepreneurship is not simply

---

[21] Barkham, R., G. Gudgin, M. Hart, and E. Hanvey. 1996. *The Determinants of Small Firm Growth: An Inter-Regional Study in the United Kingdom 1986–90, Regional Policy and Development Series 12*, 37. London: Jessica Kingsley Publishers and Regional Studies Association.

[22] Storey, D. 1994. *Understanding the Small Business Sector*, 157. London: Routledge.

discovering a "bright idea" but rather is the entire continuous process of collecting and organizing the necessary resources, identifying the best opportunities for quickly executing the idea, and then organizing the resources in a way that is best suited to take advantage of those opportunities. Studies focusing on the relationship between strategy and success for companies targeting rapid expansion have identified the following factors as being extremely important to predicting how well the business will operate: the specific functional strategies and skills of the company, particularly in areas of marketing and production; the level of technology usage and expertise; and the quality of the infrastructure created by the firm to penetrate and exploit new markets. Harrison and Taylor, in their study of "super growth" companies, identified the following key "winning performance factors": competing on quality rather than pricing; domination of a market niche; competing based on areas of strength; implementation of tight financial and operating controls; and frequent product or service innovation.[23] Levie made a similar finding in a survey that demonstrated that sustained growth was more likely to occur when a firm elected to follow a narrow market entry strategy in a rapidly growing market or industry as opposed to attempting broader strategies in markets or industries that had matured.[24] Other research in this area highlights the importance and positive impact of production focus and exceptional customer service.[25]

Another approach to evaluating how strategic decisions relate to the success of a firm is illustrated by research conducted by Accenture on how "business success" should be defined.[26] The researchers began by looking at the following five key quantitative and qualitative dimensions of

[23] Harrison, J., and B. Taylor. 1996. *Super Growth Companies: Entrepreneurs in Action*. Oxford: Butterworth-Heinnemann.

[24] Levie, J. 1995. "Strategies for New Venture Growth and Harvest: A Five Year Follow-Up of 176 Young Growing Firms in Denmark, Ireland and Scotland." *Frontiers of Entrepreneurship Research*. Wellesley, MA: Babson College.

[25] Baum, J. 1995. "On the Relation of Traits, Competencies, Motivation, Strategy and Structure to Venture Growth." *Frontiers of Entrepreneurship Research*. Wellesley, MA: Babson College.

[26] Breene, T., and P. Nunes. 2006. "Going the Distance: How the World's Best Companies Achieve High Performance." *Outlook Journal*.

business performance of larger firms over a seven-year period, all of which were also compared against a carefully selected set of competitors: growth, as measured by expansion of revenues over the measurement period; profitability, as measured by the different between the company's return on capital and its cost of capital; positioning for the future, as represented by what the researchers refer to as "future value"—the portion of the company's share price that cannot be explained by its current earnings—and by the portion of the industry total that each company's future value represents; longevity, as measured by the duration of out-performance in total return to shareholders; and consistency, as measured by the number of years during the measurement period that the company exceeded the median level of profitability, growth, and positioning for the future within its group of competitors.

The researchers acknowledged that the relative importance of the five high performance measures might vary from industry-to-industry and that care should be taken before attempting to make comparisons between firms that are not part of the same peer group of competitors. Nonetheless, they felt it was also possible to identify the following three drivers of performance, or "competitive essence," that were applicable to firms across industry boundaries:

- Market focus and position, which means knowing "where and how to compete" and successfully scaling the business by adroitly exiting mature markets and consistently identifying new markets and entering them on a timely basis;
- Distinctive capabilities, which includes the unique set of business processes and resources that cost-effectively serve the specific needs of customers (referred to by the researchers as "differentiation on the outside and simplification on the inside"); and
- Performance anatomy, which begins with a set of stable values developed by the leaders of the company and continues with the constant use and communication of those values to create a shared mindset within the company regarding critical organizational elements such as the balance between strategy and execution; the cultivation of talent; the strategic importance

of information technology; the need to measure performance selectively; and the drive for continuous innovation and renewal.

Also interesting was the observation that an apparent condition for aspiring to become a high-performance business (although not a guarantee that the level of performance will actually be achieved) is world-class excellence across the whole range of key functional areas and cross-functional activities (e.g., supply chain management; human performance; customer relationship management; finance and performance management; strategy; and information technology).

As with much of the research in this area, Accenture focused on large companies and thus the applicability of the conclusions to emerging companies is not completely clear but for the fact that emerging companies, almost by definition, aspire to become world leaders at some point in the future. Four concepts do, however, are interesting for founders and senior managers of emerging companies—creating "future value," mastering market focus and position; identifying and cultivating one or more distinctive capabilities; and laying the foundation for a strong performance anatomy. By appreciating the ultimate importance of these activities at an early stage, the leaders of an emerging company can consciously invest their time and company resources in pursuit of the goals that will pay the largest dividends in the future. This means, for example, establishing a solid infrastructure for evaluating market trends and customer needs and fostering a culture that encourages personal development and growth and innovation.

External Factors

Some researchers argue that external, or contextual, factors are the most important when considering the chances of success for a particular entrepreneurial venture or governmental policies that are intended to provide support for new business activities. These factors include such things as governmental support; market and cultural factors in the home country of the firm; industry characteristics, including the stage of development and nature of the customer base; location and market sector; and the competitive structure of the industry and the place of the firm therein as measured by its comparative advantages in relation to current and potential competitors. Bruno and Tyebjee were among the first to create an extensive list of external factors that they found to be important supports for entrepreneurial activity: venture capital availability; presence of experienced entrepreneurs; a technically skilled labor force; accessibility to suppliers; accessibility to customers or new markets; favorable government policies; proximity to universities; availability of land and facilities; accessibility to transportation; a receptive population; availability of supporting professional services; and attractive living conditions.[27] If the importance of external factors is recognized then it follows that a key determinant of the success of a new venture is the ability of the founders and other senior members of the management team to establish the appropriate strategy for handling uncertainty in their external environment and identify and acquiring the necessary resources from that environment.

Challenges for Managing Emerging Companies

Several researchers have carefully studied the progress of firms that appear to have the potential for rapid growth—emerging companies—in an attempt to identify some of the specific challenges that those firms and their managers can expect to encounter and the strategies that are most likely to be successful in overcoming those challenges. Some of the challenges are primarily related to the personal situations of the founders and the other members of the senior management team such as the lack of adequate management time, inadequacies in management skills, and conflicts within the management group. A shortage of necessary resources, such as qualified labor and/or suitable financing for expansion and credit facilities, was also often problematic. Interestingly, managers of growing firms apparently were relatively unconcerned about competition or lack of demand, both of which are consistently identified as significant

---

[27] Bruno, A., and T. Tyebjee. 1982. "The Environment for Entrepreneurship." In *Encyclopedia of Entrepreneurship*, eds. C. Kent, D. Sexton, and K. Vesper, 288. Englewood Cliffs, NJ: Prentice Hall.

challenges by managers of firms suffering through static or declining patterns. However, any new firm must anticipate that it will need to overcome certain barriers to entry and work hard to establish a reputation and track record.[28]

Hendrickson and Psarouthakis[29] identified the following eight issues that they believe must be managed in order for firms to realize growth-oriented objectives:

- **Resource Acquisition**: How does the firm acquire the necessary capital, human resources, assets, and information to launch and operate the business?
- **Resource Allocation**: How does the firm best deploy its accumulated resources?
- **Work Flow**: How are the required work activities of the business to be divided and organized to ensure efficiency and effective communications?
- **Human Relations**: How does the firm motivate and satisfy its human resources and encourage employees to understand and share a common vision?
- **Technical Mastery**: How does the firm achieve and maintain the necessary technical know-how to attain the highest levels of productivity and quality?
- **Market Strategy**: How does the firm identify its market niche and determine who its customers are and what they are looking for in making their purchasing decisions?
- **Public Relations**: What external groups, other than suppliers and customers, are important to the firm's future and what strategies should be adopted for dealing with those groups?

---

[28] Barkham, R., G. Gudgin, M. Hart, and E. Hanvey. 1996. *The Determinants of Small Firm Growth: An Inter-Regional Study in the United Kingdom 1986–90, Regional Policy and Development Series 12.* London: Jessica Kingsley Publishers and Regional Studies Association.

[29] Hendrickson, L., and J. Psarouthakis. 1998. *Dynamic Management of Growing Firms: A Strategic Approach*, 2nd ed. Ann Arbor, MI: University of Michigan Press.

- **Financial Viability**: Can the firm meet its financial obligations as they come due, grow its asset base, and operate profitably?

Achieving each of these objectives requires its own strategy and the day-to-day activities of managers and employees within the company can be understood as essential elements in pursuing each of those strategies. For example, recruitment of new employees is part of the company's resource acquisition strategy and compensation and benefit planning is part of the company's resource allocation strategy. The company's work flow strategy will be impacted and defined by decisions on job design and descriptions. Communications with employees in the form of meetings, manuals, policies, and newsletters are an integral part of the company's human relations strategy. Training and development programs are important to several different issues. Training of sales and marketing personnel can advance market strategy, while technical training should improve the company's technical mastery. In addition, training for managers should assist them in motivating employees (i.e., human relations) and smoothing work flow.

Embracing Challenges to Create a Compelling Story for Investors

While in practice it is difficult to draw lines between each of the issues listed above, they do provide a starting point for analyzing the needs of a new business and communicating a story to potential investors. For example, entrepreneurs need to be able to explain to investors what will be needed in terms of capital, human resources, assets, and information in order for the business to be successfully launched and operated. While presumably investors are being contacted to address the capital requirements of the business, the money won't be forthcoming unless the investors are satisfied about the entrepreneur's plans for acquiring the right people and technology and are convinced that the entrepreneur has the skills necessary to deploy and manage the human and technological resources so that milestones in the business plan can be achieved on a timely basis. Entrepreneurs often lack the details that investors require with respect to how the money will be spent and have difficulty explaining to investors how they intend to organize work activities, motivate their employees, and achieve the level of technical mastery necessary to create high quality products and services. In order to avoid problems, entrepreneurs need to go beyond head count projections and be prepared to show investors how the new company's critical first product development project will be managed. While sophisticated investors will understand that things don't always go as planned, they will be interested in how the entrepreneur approaches and explains the development process and will want to understand the key assumptions that the entrepreneur is making and how they are impacting the timetables and budgets in the new company's business plan.

Common Problems Confronting Emerging Companies During Start-Up

The period immediately following the initial launch of an emerging company, the so-called "start-up" phase is particularly critical for the ultimate survival of the business and calls for keen management skills and, in many cases, a dose of good fortune. Slatter identified the following as being among the most common problems confronting technology-based companies during the start-up stage: delays in product development; premature market entry; incorrect customer and market identification; lack of credibility with potential customers; unrealistic delivery promises; and lack of control over subcontractors.[30] A comprehensive review of the literature by Kazanjian to assess the relation of dominant problems to stages of growth in technology-based businesses identified the following factors as being particularly important during the start-up phase[31]:

- **Organizational Systems**: This factor included the need to develop financial systems and internal controls, as well as management information systems, and define responsibilities within the firm.

---

[30] Slatter, S. 1992. *Gambling on Growth: How to Manage the Small High-Tech Firm*, 61–68. Chichester, UK: John Wiley & Sons.

[31] Kazanjian, R. 1988. "Relation of Dominant Problems to Stages of Growth in Technology-based New Ventures." *Academy of Management Journal* 31, no. 2, pp. 257–79.

- **Sales/Marketing**: This factor focused on attainment of sales, profit and market share goals, penetration of new geographic markets, and development of product service and support.
- **People**: This factor emphasized the need to recruit capable personnel; however, no reference was made to culture and employee satisfaction and morale issues.
- **Production**: This factor covered the ability of the firm to improve the procurement and production functions to the point where sufficient volume could be generated to meet customer demand.
- **Strategic Positioning**: This factor included development of new product or technology applications and entry into new product market segments.
- **External Relations**: This factor included relationships with capital providers, as well as recruitment of outside professional advisors and board members.

Another way to identify problems is to learn more about why emerging companies failed to realize their potential and achieve the aspirations the founders had in mind when the business was first launched. Mottram acknowledged that emerging companies are, by nature, risky ventures that are highly likely to fail; however, he argued that based on his experience in working with emerging companies the founders frequently engaged in a common set of behaviors that doomed their firms yet could have been avoided or mitigated. In an effort to warn founders of challenges that may ultimately overwhelm them Mottram listed and described "10 Reasons Why Emerging Companies Fail" in a blog post that first appeared in 2009[32]:

- **Myopic or extraneous market research**: The failure of the founders to validate their ideas using basic qualitative and quantitative market research using assumptions that have

---

[32] Mottram, B. 2009. "10 Reasons Why Emerging Technology Companies Fail." *Storagetopics (blog)*. http://storagetopics.com/2009/07/why-technology-products-fail.html (accessed November 6, 2014).

been developed to avoid any bias which might influence the data and predetermine the outcome. Faulty research leads to poor business and marketing planning and strategies based on the founder's personal experiences rather than hard data from the actual marketplace itself.

- **Product development guided by internal perceptions and biases**: Founders need to remember that a new technology, regardless of how innovative it might be, is of little use to customers unless it provides them with a cost-effective solution to a real problem they are facing and provides them with a new way to increase their profits and/or become and remain more competitive.

- **Overly optimistic marketing plans**: Founders should certainly develop a marketing plan that creates enthusiasm within their team; however, care should be taken not to become too optimistic and pursue goals that are unrealistic and set the stage for failure and deterioration of morale and scarce resources.

- **Incomplete product**: Founders need to remember that customers evaluate products, particularly technology-based products, on the basis of the entire customer experience and not just a particular feature or function. Accordingly, product development needs to be seen expansively and include installation, training, financing, technical support, application support, application ecosystem, and customer comfort with the company's reputation in the marketplace. The goal should be to build and maintain a brand not just a commodity product or service.

- **Undifferentiated products**: Founders must be sure that their new products can be easily differentiated by prospective customers and that the point of differentiation is considered meaningful by customers and not just the founders and their team members. Following on the point above, founders need to remember that customers look at their entire experience and there are opportunities for differentiation that are outside the familiar issues of features and pricing.

- **Weak or confused market focus:** While founders are eager and anxious to generate sales revenues as quickly as possible care must be taken to avoid weak or confused market focus and marketing efforts should be directed toward niches and segments that offer the best opportunities for success. Many companies fail because they chase any new sales possibility regardless of whether it will be profitable or whether it makes sense in the long-term and the result is that scarce resources are overextended and support costs increase over the original budget.

- **Vague messaging and poor positioning:** Founders need to avoid getting caught up in their own excitement and take the time to sit down and calmly and objectively develop a clear statement and argument for customers regarding the value of the new product or service as a solution for customer problems and position the product or service in a way that allows customers to easily differentiate it in a noisy and competitive marketplace.

- **Channel confusion:** Once again, in their pursuit of quick sales founders often neglect to take the time to develop a coherent channel strategy. The founders need to take the time to make the tough choices among direct, indirect, and combination sales strategies and then closely manage each of the channels to avoid conflicts and ensure that each channel is being pursued effectively.

- **Executive thinking that promotion is marketing:** Founders and other senior executives of emerging companies often believe that marketing has only one goal: generating demand for the company's products and services. While demand generation is important, emerging companies cannot ignore the need to build the company's reputation and brand, both of which are essential to the long-term success and sustainability of the firm.

- **Marketing and sales teams disconnected:** Founders need to act carefully and thoughtfully as they distinguish and build out the marketing and sales teams and make sure that there is communication and coordination between the functions in key areas such as identifying segmentation and target customers, development and implementation of "go-to-market" strategies, channel strategies, lead generation and qualification, sales tools and training.

Several years later in 2014, Mottram restated his original list and added a few more potential problems outside of his original focus on marketing and sales issues including the following: lack of passion and persistence among company leadership; dysfunction, including conflicting agendas, among the leadership team; operational mediocrity and inefficiencies; inability to think and act fast: being too dogmatic and thus unable or unwilling to react to market changes; lack of mentors or advisors; insufficient funding; unprofitable or no business model; over-expansion; poor launch strategy and lack of coherence within the launch team; and an idea that is not scalable.[33] While Mottram's catalog is extensive, founders must be mindful of the need to overcome other challenges such as poor cash management skills, failure to create a well-developed business plan, poor pricing strategies, unwillingness or inability to recognize areas in which they need help from others, failure to delegate, poor hiring decisions (i.e., hiring people that think the same way as the founder as opposed to people with different viewpoints and complementary skills and experience), failure to understand and pay attention to the competition and too much reliance on a single customer.

Milestones for Change and Transition Within Emerging Companies

There have been a number of attempts to identify the stages of development of a business and recognizing and accepting that change and evolution is inevitable is essential to the pursuit of continuous success and survival for the enterprise. There is no universally accepted growth model

---

[33] Mottram B. 2014. "Revisiting a Popular Post: '10 Reasons Why Technology Companies Fail.'" *Storagetopics (blog)*. http://storagetopics.com/2014/07/why-companies-fail.html (accessed November 6, 2014).

for emerging companies; however, it is clear that as time goes by there will be changes in immediate business objectives, predominant management style, organizational structure, the state of the company company's product and market activities and the most pressing managerial challenges (e.g., resource management, sales and marketing, and communications and cooperation within the organization). For example, Hendrickson and Psarouthakis have provided a useful and comprehensive list of some of the milestones that tend to trigger the need for change within firms that have experienced rapid growth:

- As the firm grows, resource acquisition priorities shift from capital to recruiting qualified and experienced managerial and technical employees.
- In the marketing area, growing companies may find that they can no longer fulfill their appetite for expansion in a small niche that allowed the company to launch successfully. As a result, the firm must adopt more formal strategic planning methods to locate and attack new markets and/or develop new products or services.
- As the business grows and becomes more complex, senior managers must be more mindful of outside constituencies and requirements, particularly laws and regulations that come into play as the firm increases in size and the number of customers and other business partners expands.
- As the customer base expands and orders rise, the company must learn to carefully manage its available resources. The simple and basic internal controls that were adequate when the firm had only a handful of customers must be replaced by formal budgets and computerized accounting.
- The need for the firm to expand into new markets and service more customers tends to lead to more specialization among managers and employees. This not only impacts the way in which the company must recruit and select new employees, it also creates challenges of communication to make sure that tasks and activities do not overlap.

- Employee growth and increased specialization inevitably lead to great distance between the founders and professional senior executives, such as the CEO, and other parts of the organization. As a result, it becomes most difficult for the CEO to keep an eye on the pulse of the firm and directly and clearly convey his or her sense of company mission to employees.
- The need for advanced internal controls, standardized products, and enhanced product quality and productivity means that the firm must focus on improving technical mastery through recruitment of new employees and ongoing training of current workers.

Of course, the CEO of every firm, regardless of its goals and expectations with respect to growth, may need to initiate changes that are unrelated to the challenges described above. For example, change may be triggered by recognition that a current strategy or approach is no longer effective or that it is no longer sufficient to attempt to operate without formally addressing a particular issue; the need to seize an opportunity to make improvements in the way that the firm may already be dealing with a particular issue, such as increasing efficiencies and further reducing costs; or the need to respond to major changes in structure or other internal circumstances, such as a significant change in the number of employees, diversification, acquisitions, or the departure of one of more key senior managers.

Responding to these challenges requires specific actions by the founders and other members of the senior management team of an emerging company including development of the proper strategies for recruiting employees with proper technical skills and experience; proper design and implementation of corporate budgeting and planning systems; establishment of an efficient purchasing and production systems to ensure that products can be manufactured in a timely manner and at desired levels of quality; development of strategies for creating a loyal and satisfied group of employees, including training and skill development programs to build and maintain technical mastery; and proper investment of time and other resources in market research and new product development to create products and services that address an identifiable customer demand. While the solutions can often be readily identified actual execution may be hampered by resistance to change, shortcomings in diagnosing the causes of the particular problem or issue, inappropriate solutions and failure to adequately measure and evaluate the results of the change in relation to the situation that existed in the past.[34]

Other surveys and research efforts over the years have provided additional insights and perspective on challenges confronting emerging companies. For example, a study of a group of Inc. 100 companies in the early 1980s identified the following crucial transformation issues that must be overcome in order for firms to be successful in their growth plans: acquisition of management resources, both at the executive level and at middle management, development of work flow systems, human relations and cultivation of firm culture, and resource allocation.[35] In addition, interviews of CEOs of 121 Inc. 500 companies conducted in the early 1990s identified the following as key problems that arise as the firm moves beyond the start-up stage and into the period where rapid growth is anticipated: obtaining adequate capital, raw materials, and human resources; controlling margins, expenses, and cash flow and developing sufficient production capacity; modifying allocation of job responsibilities, transitioning from customized to standardized products, and training and development of workers; building employee satisfaction and morale and reducing turnover; developing technical expertise and integrating it into product development and production processes; and building a broader customer base and developing new marketing and distribution channels.[36] The researchers also identified lack of management time and

---

[34] Hendrickson, L., and J. Psarouthakis. 1998. *Dynamic Management of Growing Firms: A Strategic Approach*, 2nd ed. Ann Arbor, MI: University of Michigan Press.

[35] Hambrick, D., and L. Crozier. 1985. "Stumblers and Stars in the Management of Rapid Growth." *Journal of Business Venturing* 1, no. 1, pp. 31–45.

[36] Terpstra, D., and P. Olson. 1993. "Entrepreneurial Start-up and Growth: A Classification of Problems." *Entrepreneurship Theory and Practice* 17, no. 3, pp. 5–20.

expertise as an important issue that tended to contribute to the challenges in each of the areas listed above.

Strategic Alternatives for Emerging Companies

While an extensive discussion of strategic alternatives for emerging companies is beyond the scope of this chapter it is useful to understand the different categories of strategies that have been identified for these types of companies. New companies may select from among a number of identifiable strategies when identifying their initial activities. Each activity has its own level of risk and resource requirements and the appropriate mix of activities will depend on a variety of factors. For example, relatively low risk activities that may be completed with a limited set of resources include technology consulting, contract research work, and development of custom and semi-custom niche products. Pursuit of these activities may be appropriate in cases where the ultimate market for the company's products and technology is still emerging and final direction is difficult to predict. On the other hand, development of standardized products for potentially large markets is a much higher risk activity that will require substantially more resources, including capital to allow the firm to survive until the development is completed and the product is launched. A strategy based on these activities should be considered when the firm is confident about the technology and the size of the market. In some cases, the firm has little choice but to proceed in this direction if the company's internal technology base is so narrow that it is impractical to try and take on a diverse set of consulting and niche development projects.

Assuming that the business concept underlying the new firm is based on commercialization of a "radical" technological innovation the first step will normally be adaptation of the technology to an identified need in the marketplace and educating potential customers about the technology and the ways in which it can be used to solve a specific problem of importance to the customer base. The activities of the firm at this stage have been characterized as "research and consultancy" and the company will often engage focused contract activities to diffuse knowledge about the commercial applications of the technology, as opposed to ramping up for large-scale production of standardized products. In many ways, the firm and its products are still "soft" at this stage and changes may be made as a result of information gained during the consultation activities. The next stages of development may include distribution of the company's proprietary products by other companies and eventually creation of the company's own independent functions for manufacturing and marketing.

One strategy used by emerging companies is referred to as "focused" and contemplates that the firm will attempt to secure a dominant position in a specific market niche. A more "broad-based" strategy emphasizes introduction of the technology into a wide range of products and industries, often through joint ventures and other strategic alliance with third parties. Some companies opt for an "early product" strategy based on rapid introduction of new products into markets with low barriers to entry and relatively small consultancy costs. This strategy is generally followed when the firm is looking to generate cash quickly in order to continue to finance development of more sophisticated products that can be launched using one of the other strategies. If, for whatever reason, the firm is destined to pursue the riskier path of developing a full-fledged line of standardized products, consideration should be given to various strategies that can be used to manage those risks and keep the company moving forward until a return on the large investment can be realized. Among the possibilities are the following:

- Companies may gain experience with some of the activities related to development and commercialization of their selected products by providing manufacturing, distribution, or service for similar products designed by other manufacturers. These projects not only build the knowledge base of the firm, but also can provide cash flow that can be used to continue the product development effort and begin building the necessary support functions.
- Complementing the standardized products with additional offerings of customized versions that are built to meet the specific requirements of various market segments within the broader product class.
- Entering into large contracts with one or more customers to provide a specified volume of products. These types of

contracts with key customers, particularly customers that are perceived as important players in the target market, can provide a steady stream of revenues and also create opportunities for the firm to improve its manufacturing and service functions. The downside is that these large contracts may derail the firm from pursuing its primary product development objectives. Moreover, in some cases, restrictions in such contracts make it difficult for the firm to expand its customer network.

- Entering into "private label" or OEM contracts can provide benefits similar to those associated with large customer contracts, notably cash flow.

The success of the selected strategy will depend, to some degree, on the reaction from established competitors. A variety of scenarios are possible, including attempts to improve existing technologies to reduce the innovative appeal of the products offered by the start-up firm or an effort by incumbents to secure technological leadership by either creating similar products at lower prices or moving forward with development of second generation products. Efforts to attain technological leadership are generally facilitated by the fact that incumbent firms are typically larger and already have an integrated functional structure that includes development, manufacturing, and distribution. Start-up firms confronted by this type of opposition face greater challenges in surviving long enough to become an independent and fully functioning entity and are often forced into acquisition, termination, or continuation as a small niche player supporting the larger firms. A well-known example of this type of reaction can be found in a review of the early years of the biotechnology revolution. As small firms began to emerge, large incumbents in many industries, including agricultural, chemicals, and pharmaceuticals, responded by making large investment in traditional technologies and in biotechnological research itself. It should be noted that the optimal situation for growth is probably somewhere between these two extremes, since small innovative firms will need industry cooperation, in the form of financing and marketing arrangements, to continue to grow.

About the Author

Dr Alan S. Gutterman is the Founding Director of the Sustainable Entrepreneurship Project (www.seproject.org). In addition, Alan's prolific output of practical guidance and tools for legal and financial professionals, managers, entrepreneurs, and investors has made him one of the best-selling individual authors in the global legal publishing marketplace. His cornerstone work, *Business Transactions Solution*, is an online-only product available and featured on Thomson Reuter's Westlaw, the world's largest legal content platform, which includes almost 200 book-length modules covering the entire lifecycle of a business. Alan has also authored or edited over 40 books on sustainable entrepreneurship, management, business law and transactions, international law business and technology management for a number of publishers including Thomson Reuters, Kluwer, Aspatore, Oxford, Quorum, ABA Press, Aspen, Sweet & Maxwell, Euromoney, CCH, and BNA. Alan has over three decades of experience as a partner and senior counsel with internationally recognized law firms counselling small and large business enterprises in the areas of general corporate and securities matters, venture capital, mergers and acquisitions, international law and transactions, strategic business alliances, technology transfers, and intellectual property, and has also held senior management positions with several technology-based businesses including service as the chief legal officer of a leading international distributor of IT products headquartered in Silicon Valley and as the chief operating officer of an emerging broadband media company. He has been an adjunct faculty member at several colleges and universities, including Boalt Hall, Golden Gate University, Hastings College of Law, Santa Clara University, and the University of San Francisco, teaching classes on a diverse range of topics including corporate finance, venture capital, corporate law, Japanese business law, and law and economic development, He received his AB, MBA, and JD from the University of California at Berkeley, a DBA from Golden Gate University, and a PhD from the University of Cambridge. For more information about Alan, his publications, or the Sustainable Entrepreneurship Project, please contact him directly at alangutterman@gmail.com, and follow him on LinkedIn (https://linkedin.com/in/alangutterman/).

Index

OTHER TITLES IN THE ENTREPRENEURSHIP AND SMALL BUSINESS MANAGEMENT COLLECTION

Scott Shane, Case Western University, Editor

- *Open Innovation Essentials for Small and Medium Enterprises: A Guide to Help Entrepreneurs in Adopting the Open Innovation Paradigm in Their Business* by Luca Escoffier, Adriano La Vopa, Phyllis Speser, and Daniel Satinsky
- *The Technological Entrepreneur's Playbook* by Ian Chaston
- *Licensing Myths & Mastery: Why Most Ideas Don't Work and What to Do About It* by William S. Seidel
- *Arts and Entrepreneurship* by J. Mark Munoz and Julie Shields
- *The Human Being's Guide to Business Growth: A Simple Process for Unleashing the Power of Your People for Growth* by Gregory Scott Chambers
- *Understanding the Family Business: Exploring the Differences Between Family and Nonfamily Businesses, Second Edition* by Keanon J. Alderson

Announcing the Business Expert Press Digital Library

Concise e-books business students need for classroom and research

This book can also be purchased in an e-book collection by your library as

- a one-time purchase,
- that is owned forever,
- allows for simultaneous readers,
- has no restrictions on printing, and
- can be downloaded as PDFs from within the library community.

Our digital library collections are a great solution to beat the rising cost of textbooks. E-books can be loaded into their course management systems or onto students' e-book readers.
The **Business Expert Press** digital libraries are very affordable, with no obligation to buy in future years. For more information, please visit **www.businessexpertpress.com/librarians**. To set up a trial in the United States, please email **sales@businessexpertpress.com**.